The
FINANCIAL
PLANNING
PUZZLE

Fitting Your Pieces Together
to Create Financial Freedom

JASON SILVERBERG

CFP®, CLU®, ChFC®

Silverstone
Press

Jason is a registered representative and investment advisor representative of Securian Financial Services, Inc. Member FINRA/SIPC. Financial Advantage Associates, Inc. is independently owned and operated. For more information, contact Jason at 301-610-0071 or jason@finadvinc.com. 1561171 DOFU 1/2017.

Published by Silverstone Press, LLC.
Edited by Leslie Watts
Formatted by Perry Elisabeth Design
ISBN 978-0-9980775-0-5 (Hardcover)
ISBN 978-0-9980775-1-2 (eBook)
ISBN 978-0-9980775-2-9 (Audiobook)

10 9 8 7 6 5 4 3 2 1

Dedication

To my children, Joshua and Rebecca,
who have filled my life with joy and purpose.

To my wife, Lindsay,
who has always been by my side on the rollercoaster of life.

To my parents, Fred and Carol,
who, whether on purpose or not, shaped who I am today.

To my brothers, Scott and Steven,
who have always been there to keep me in check.

I thank you all for your love and support!

- Jason Silverberg

Table of Contents

Foreword

I first met Jason Silverberg in 2006 when he was fairly new to his career. I worked with Jason and Financial Advantage (the firm he was an advisor in) and helped them grow their practice by applying a set of structures so that they could execute more consistently.

I've come to realize that success in life is not a matter of knowledge, intellect, or information. It's not a new strategy or idea. It's not contingent on a large network of connected people. It's not predicated on hard work, natural talent, or luck. In the end, accomplishing one's goals and dreams comes down to execution. It's simply not enough to know or have access to resources; it's all about the implementation.

Financial success is no different. That is what I like about what Jason has put together in *The Financial Planning Puzzle*. Book stores are full of a lot of books on how to handle your finances, build wealth, and secure your future. What is different with this book is Jason's grounding in the concepts of execution.

In *The Financial Planning Puzzle*, Jason walks you through the various aspects of your financial life. He takes you step-by-step, as your financial coach, through all the facets of financial planning without overwhelming you. Jason will help you understand the what, why, and how of your financial life. He provides everything you need to take control of your finances and, most importantly, take action.

Building a financial plan doesn't need to be complicated or arduous. As Jason outlines, it all starts with the vision of what you want. Then you can break that down into bite-size pieces that are manageable and doable.

As you execute your plan, you will encounter some challenges and setbacks. If you stay the course, the rewards are destined to come. Focus on the actions, not the outcomes. In the end, you control the actions, not the results. The more consistent you are with the actions, the greater the probability of achieving the desired outcomes.

The Financial Planning Puzzle is a book you can open to any chapter and find valuable insights and practical actions you can put into practice today. Read this book. Study it. Apply it!

Best wishes,

Brian P. Moran
CEO & Founder of the 12 Week Year™
New York Times Bestselling Author

Preface

At some point, you've put a puzzle together with a friend or family member. You most likely had fun with this activity, but might have also experienced some frustration. Starting out with a clear strategy could provide a better outcome.

Maybe you decide to start out looking for the four corner pieces, and then move on to the end pieces. You might also decide to group like colors and patterns together. It would also be helpful to consult the picture on the puzzle box as a guide. Whatever strategy you choose, you'll go in with a thoughtful process that will provide you a better chance of success.

Merriam-Webster defines the word *puzzle* as "a question or problem that requires thought, skill, or cleverness to be answered or solved." Your financial life can be compared to that puzzle, where thought, skill, and cleverness are integral in putting it all together to achieve success. That's where this book can help.

I wrote *The Financial Planning Puzzle* to help people understand that putting your financial puzzle together doesn't need to be so hard. With a proper understanding of the picture on the box, each puzzle piece's unique characteristics, and how everything fits together, you will be on your way to achieving your financial goals and being *on purpose* with your money.

Writing this book has been quite the journey. You could say it was a puzzle in itself. I started out by writing what came to mind. Next, I tried to organize the book into a preliminary structure. I divided the content into three parts that explain why a financial plan makes sense.

I found my muse along the way and hit my stride about halfway through. I pieced my prior writings together and filled in the gaps. After countless edits and changes, I finally had a finished product.

I've learned a lot along the way. Many of the concepts in this book actually apply to my writing experience. For example, there was a chapter I wrote that I needed to discard, much like an investment that isn't the right fit. I didn't want to let ego get in the way of success.

I wrote this book for many different types of people. The newlywed couple laying the foundation for their financial lives. The new parent who feels overwhelmed with sleepless nights and has competing financial priorities. The small business owner balancing business and personal financial challenges. The divorcee, who is starting over and feeling discouraged by how far they've fallen behind. The pre-retiree who's worried about living without a paycheck for the rest of their lives. And the federal employee who seeks to maximize their benefits through work. Ultimately, this book is for anyone who would like to improve their financial lives.

Keep in mind that this book is not meant to be a substitute for a financial advisor. Nobody but your financial advisor should be giving you specific financial advice. Be sure to hire one that can speak to your specific financial circumstances.

Acknowledgments

I wish to personally thank the following people for their inspiration, knowledge, and guidance in making this book the best it can be:

My parents, Carol and Fred Silverberg, and my in-laws, Deborah and Charles Firestone. Thank you for your support and encouragement in creating this book, as well as reviewing the numerous edits with critiques and criticism.

My mentors Jonathan Abbett and John Gracyalny. Thank you for countless hours of training, coaching, and motivation.

My editor, Leslie Watts. Thank you for your tough love with the red pen.

My clients and those whom I have helped. Thank you for placing your trust with me to help you attain your financial dreams and goals.

My friends, Matthew Bernstein, Mark Nadel, Brian Wasser, Micah Bender, Adam Abramowitz, Hirsh Goldberg, and Brian Banks. Thank you for pushing me to strive for excellence.

My grandparents, Joseph and Elaine Chucker and Sol and Shirley Silverberg. Thank you for your encouragement and wisdom on my lifelong pursuit of being a money maven.

My brothers, Scott and Steven Silverberg. Thank you for hours of nonsensical, back-and-forth banter that helped me debate both sides of any argument.

My wife, Lindsay Silverberg, and children, Joshua and Rebecca Silverberg. Thank you for the unconditional love, hugs, and joy you bring into my life. You inspire me each day to be the best version of myself so I can set an example for you. I love you all.

The Financial Planning Puzzle

Introduction
My Story

Coins. What kid doesn't love them? They're shiny and colorful and fun to toss around. As a child, I obsessed over coins. Rolling coins with my Dad was the highlight of my week. My rare penny collection also taught me some interesting facts. Did you know that the US Mint used to make pennies out of steel? During World War II, copper was scarce due to the war effort. In my childhood, coins were everywhere. But what did they mean? What was their purpose? How did they work? These questions sparked my lifelong relationship with money.

Childhood

Growing up, I was aware of money, even at an early age. From the coin counting book I read in kindergarten to playing dreidel with my family at Hanukkah. Money was something integral to my family, but I had a hunch it meant something bigger as well. I just didn't have the right perspective to grasp how big.

My parents were pretty transparent about money and what it meant to our family. My dad worked full-time while my mom stayed at home. Pizza on Friday nights was a big deal. When we ate out at a restaurant, appetizers and desserts were always forbidden. It was a real treat to have a soft drink with our meal, but it had to come with free refills. We weren't poor, just your typical middle-class family.

My brothers and I took on housekeeping chores in exchange for a $2 per week allowance. We didn't actually receive the cash, but rather kept track of our payables on the computer. Once my accrued earnings had accumulated into a large enough lump sum, my dad would pay me out. My friend down the street used to get $5 per week for fewer chores, which seemed unfair. I shared this with my parents, and they came back with the typical parental retorts. I made a mental note of this for later.

I had this burning desire to earn income in new ways. One day, I was taking a break from mowing the lawn, and it dawned on me. *Why am I mowing only this patch of grass when there is grass up and down both sides of the street?* This was the genesis of my first business venture. I knocked on doors and put up signs. I knew I was onto something when I received my first job. My business scaled out to cutting four different lawns that summer. I made more money than any of my other 12-year-old friends. It was hard work but definitely made me feel good about myself.

Around age 13, I had my Bar Mitzvah. It was a turning point in my childhood. This monumental occasion represents a Jewish boy's journey into manhood. I needed to learn my Hebrew verses and speak them in front of my family and friends. The reward was a big party and gifts, and maybe even some money.

My sights were set on a state-of-the-art stereo system with a dual cassette deck and a three-CD carousel changer. Although, as a 13-year-old, my biggest reward was the relief of completion. No more extra tutoring, late night practice sessions, or added pressure. Looking back, this was the first time I struggled and persevered. It solidified the foundation for my work ethic.

The eventful day came and went and my loved ones were generous with their gifts. My parents helped me learn what to do with all the checks I received. I set up my first bank account, endorsed the checks, and deposited the funds. From there, my dad encouraged me to invest most of the money. Since we earmarked the money for college, a few years away, we invested in the stock market. We chose a few balanced mutual funds, and then I got to choose a stock. It had to be something I knew, something that would be the obsession of any 13-year-old growing up the 90s. It had to be Nike.

I made a little money and caught the investing bug. I couldn't believe I was able to do this. It was so much fun. I bought a couple more stocks and made more money. I couldn't lose. Until I did. Sure enough, I saw my mutual funds drop. And drop. And drop. I experienced, in my early teens, what many people don't experience until they're older: loss aversion. My parents coached me to stay invested and not to panic. After all, I didn't need the money right then.

The next day, I opened the newspaper and all my investments were up. And up they went. After that, I added a couple more stocks to my portfolio. When I got my driver's license, I decided to cash in my winnings to buy my first car.

A red 1996 Mazda Protégé. What a beauty. It wasn't just a car. It represented more than that. It was the manifestation of my hard work, late nights, careful planning, and sweat equity. I could go anywhere, do anything, and I guess had to pay for gas too.

I held a job for most of my high school years. My resume consisted of babysitting, serving frozen yogurt, developing pictures, and running a bakery. My senior year capped off with an on-the-job training program that my school offered. I left school early and worked someplace that would build out my skillset. It was a great experience and gave me a taste of what the "real world" had to offer.

Around this time, my parents struggled to make their relationship work. They decided to split up. While it was for the best, it still was hard. They argued about a variety of different things, and money was a big factor. I heard bits and pieces of their conversation, which changed my perspective. I could see how money affects a household and a relationship and how it wasn't always good.

My dad moved out, and then they were supporting two separate households. Money was tight again. My needs were always met by my parents, but my wants were a different story. I attended the University of Maryland and worked throughout school. I knew I wanted to work in a money-related field, so I took a job as a bank teller. I learned a lot about the banking system and the bigger role that money plays in the world. This was the missing piece in my understanding of money.

I did a lot of soul-searching during those years and put a lot of pressure on myself to commit to a career. I considered the role money had played in my life: the good, the bad, and the ugly. I finally determined that I wanted to help people make smart financial decisions. Financial planning was the perfect fit.

———

All my experiences have shaped who I am today. As a parent of two children, I now reflect on my childhood. I pick and choose the best aspects of the lessons that I've learned and teach my kids similar principles. I've learned a lot and still have a lot to learn. I'm looking forward to giving them, and you, the same gift my parents gave me: the gift of a financial education.

In the coming pages, you will gain a better understanding of how to manage your finances. You'll determine what financial freedom means to you and the steps to take to help you get there. I've broken the book into three sections: Part 1 - The Financial Framework will define financial planning. You'll gain an understanding of your money mindset too. Finally, we'll wrap up the first part with the challenges facing the middle class. In Part 2 – Your Financial Pieces, I'll help you look at each area of your financial world. This is where you'll get key nuggets of information to help you in your planning. You'll take these bite-size morsels with you as we move to Part 3 – Fitting the Pieces Together. In this section, we'll put it all together and I'll share some success stories.

As you read through the book, you may notice that some of the sections may not pertain to you and your specific situation. You can skip any sections that don't fit your financial plan, however it's a good idea to capture all of the foundational information in Part 2 – Your Financial Pieces.

Also, as you're reading, you might begin to feel some resistance toward some of the concepts. This is normal and I urge you to keep going. As with anything new, there may be some uncomfortably that we'll need to break through to achieve success.

Finally, don't be afraid to drop me a line and let me know what you think. You can send me an email at Jason@finadvinc.com or call me at 301-610-0071. So, if you're ready to begin the process of improving your financial life, then let's get started!

Part 1
The Financial Framework

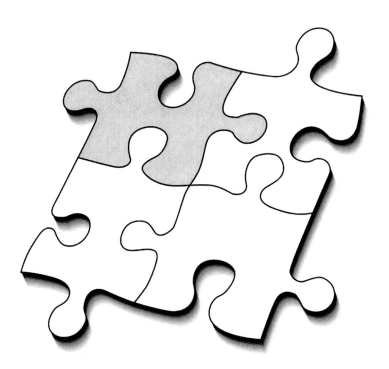

Chapter 1
Financial Flow

The zone is a state of mind which is marked by a sense of calmness. In addition, there is a heightened sense of awareness and focus. Actions seem effortless and there is an increased belief that your dreams or goals can become achievable and real. In addition, there is also a sense of deep enjoyment when the person is in this unique, special and magical state of being.
—Dr. Jay Granat, Sports Psychologist

Imagine you and your family huddled around the kitchen table, ready to tackle a 1,000-piece puzzle. You know it will be challenging but also a fun bonding experience. You open the box and dump the pieces on the table. At first the task looks overwhelming. Then you realize that you have the picture on the box to help guide you along.

If you're like most Americans, you not only have done this with a puzzle, but also your financial life. Some people try to put their puzzle together and may, in fact, be missing some pieces. They can't seem to figure out how to make it all work.

Others may have all the pieces they need but never use the picture on the box to help them complete the puzzle. What's worse is that many of us tend to use the picture on someone else's puzzle box as a guide to putting our own puzzles together. No wonder we get so frustrated.

Many people accumulate their financial puzzle pieces throughout their lives, and most times without an organized way to manage it all. You might have a 401(k) plan that's still at your old job. What about that life insurance policy you bought from your friend a long time ago? Or that IRA you've been contributing to but don't know why? After reviewing everything, you might even have duplicates of products without knowing it.

The key here is that none of these financial instruments are "talking" to each other. We don't have a clear way to assess each piece or to form a strategy that fits everything together. We need a financial plan.

What is a Financial Plan?

If you've ever taken a road trip, you've most likely gathered several items before taking off. Putting gas in your car is a must. You could have checked the oil and prepared a playlist for the ride. Also, you might have remembered a spare tire, jumper cables, or a bit of food in case you got stuck. Whatever your preparations, one thing you wouldn't leave behind is a map or a GPS.

Financial planning is exactly that—your road map! It will help you get from where you are today to where you want to be tomorrow. Your fuel for your plan includes your investment and savings strategies. Your jumper cables are your insurance policies and other risk management strategies. A well-designed financial plan should help you navigate all of life's speed bumps.

The Financial Planning Association defines financial planning as "the long-term process of wisely managing your finances so you can achieve your goals and dreams, while at the same time negotiating the financial barriers that inevitably arise in every stage of life." You may think that you have a financial plan in place. Perhaps you work with a stockbroker, an investment advisor, an insurance agent, an accountant, or even an attorney. But if you have several advisors, each might be using a different playbook and adding more confusion to your financial puzzle.

One of the reasons people create a financial plan is to receive customized advice. Financial planning provides you with the opportunity to define and prioritize your financial goals. This is something that many people never take the time to do. You'll also want to explore whether your current habits are congruent with those goals.

When you meet with your planner, you may discover new ideas that challenge your status quo. You might even wonder why you're doing what you're currently doing. You may not have a good answer, and that's okay. Many times, it's at this point when you'll want to compare yourself to a friend or loved one. As a reminder, this is your life, not theirs. Take a step back and consider the motivating force behind your own financial behaviors.

It's easy to get stuck in the minutia of the day-to-day grind and neglect to think at a high level. A 2013 Bankrate.com survey found that 76% of Americans are living paycheck to paycheck.[1] If we're stuck worrying about how to pay our bills, how can we expect to think bigger? A financial plan can mute the worry and help us to design the lives we want —on purpose.

A financial plan also illuminates how our goals are interrelated. For example, will your college savings strategy for your children compromise your ability to retire? Did you accidentally create a large tax bill for your estate with your life insurance plan? By changing one small piece of your puzzle, you can have a dramatic impact on the bigger picture.

The Financial Planning Process

The financial planning process is integral to reaching your financial goals. You begin by establishing and defining your relationship to

---

[1] Johnson, Angela. "76% of Americans Are Living Paycheck-to-paycheck." CNNMoney. June 24, 2013. Accessed December 09, 2016, http://money.cnn.com/2013/06/24/pf/emergency-savings/.

align expectations. It's important for you and your financial planner to be on the same page and that you both have the same image for the completed puzzle. The planner will gather financial data, consult with industry experts to analyze the data, and develop recommendations and action steps for you. Together, you will discuss a timetable for implementing your plan, assign responsibilities, and schedule regular meetings to monitor and evaluate progress toward your goals.

Keep in mind that financial planning is not a one-and-done process. It evolves with you. As you experience major life changes, the process may start over. You and your planner will need to discuss new information and changes to your plan. From there, you'll work together to create a new action plan.

Financial planning is a long-term process. A good financial plan may not address all your goals upfront but rather in stages or priorities. Your preferences will be factored into what's most important.

As you consider how to assign priorities, consider sketching out your goals by timeframe. One of the most pressing issues might be protecting yourself in case of catastrophe. Then you may begin to think about short-term goals, such as paying down debts, managing a budget, or buying a car.

Beyond that, you'll review your mid-term goals. These could include buying a house, taking a vacation, or saving for college. Finally, you'll want to consider long-term goals. Saving for retirement is one of the most pressing ones, but you might want to own a business or buy a second home as well. The order in which you address your goals will depend on what you and your family consider most important.

A financial plan will not allow you to delegate all your financial decisions. A planner will need some information and assistance from you in creating your tailored strategy. Also, while financial planning can assist with cash flow and budgeting, it cannot act as a substitute for legal advice if you are facing a possible bankruptcy filing. In that situation, the best step is to consult with a qualified attorney or credit specialist.

Separate from the financial plan and an advisor's role as a financial planner, your planner may recommend the purchase of specific investment or insurance products and accounts. These recommendations are not part of the financial plan, and you are under no obligation to follow them.

Living the Life You Want

While this all sounds great in theory, you might still be skeptical. Is a financial plan right for you? Below are some actual comments from people who have completed this work:

- "I now feel empowered to take on bigger goals that I thought were too far out of my reach. I can be a better me."
- "A weight has truly been lifted off my shoulders. I can now sleep easily at night knowing I have a plan in place."
- "I can now confidently manage my money and free up time to spend with my family."
- "This has given me a sense of security so I feel I can retire worry-free."
- "I can achieve my goals faster, taking less risk."

You could say that the goal of financial planning is to achieve a state of "flow" with your finances. Mihaly Csikszentmihalyi defines this concept in his book *Flow: The Psychology of Optimal Experience*. Also known as "the zone," flow is a mental state, one in which we are fully immersed in a feeling of energized focus, total involvement, and sheer enjoyment in the process of an activity. It's when our purpose, values, and actions are all in alignment.

Athletes experience this frequently. They're completely focused on the game and can drown out all the background noise. Similarly, we too need to have a laser-like focus on our financial habits and strategies. This way, nothing can distract us from achieving our goals.

We must align these goals with our purpose. Some call it a "calling" or their "life's work," but purpose can simply be something that motivates you to be the best version of yourself or help others. We can examine how money can further that purpose and actualize our ultimate financial goals.

We can use our values as the core principles in shaping our plans. These values can serve as our guideposts along the way. As an example, if your purpose is to raise your children to be healthy, happy, and self-reliant individuals, you might put a heavier weight on the goal of saving for college and teaching them about money.

Many studies have linked being in a state of "flow" to happiness. Think about how great you feel when you know what to do and you actually do it. For example, you know that you need to get into better physical shape. You decide to adjust your lifestyle to create more time at the gym. You might also opt for healthier meal choices.

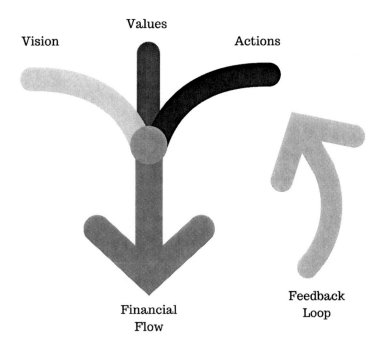

Vision   Values   Actions

Financial Flow

Feedback Loop

By aligning your thoughts, actions, and goals, you've created the financial flow you're seeking. You begin to feel proud of your discipline to stick with the plan. You've made progress toward a better life, and your goals are now more achievable. Gandhi once said, "Be the change you wish to see in the world." If you want a better life, it's yours for the making.

As you build your self-confidence, you feel happier and can think bigger. You can do more and be a better you. You end up creating a feedback loop of happiness. The energy you create by executing your plan fuels your continual progress.

While this seems so easy to do, many of us experience some major roadblocks and challenges. We may end up sabotaging our plans by giving in to our fears or anxieties. Similarly, we may think that ignorance is bliss. It's so much easier to stick our heads in the sand.

Many of us turn a blind eye toward our finances. We might do this because we don't know how to help ourselves. Or maybe we're ashamed of where we are and don't want to deal with it. Acting out of fear never creates success.

This truth is reflected in the state of most Americans' finances. According to the Statistic Brain Research Institute's August 2015 study, the average American family has just shy of $4,000 in their savings account, and 25% of Americans have no savings at all. Additionally, only 18% of those surveyed were very confident about their retirement plan.[2]

With numbers like these, the need for improvement is huge. We can either wallow in our problems or get motivated to start improving our lives. After all, we only have one life to live. Let's make it a good one.

---

[2] Harden, Seth. "American Family Financial Wealth Statistics - Statistic Brain." Statistic Brain. 2016. Accessed December 09, 2016, http://www.statisticbrain.com/american-family-financial-statistics/.

Chapter 2
Your Money Mind

Wealth is the ability to fully experience life.
—Henry David Thoreau

As with most things in life, our thoughts are at the core of any decision we make. We may make a choice consciously or unconsciously. Some decisions are well planned and deliberate, like where to go for dinner or what type of car to buy. Other decisions are made via our subconscious. How many times can you remember making the choice to brush your teeth? You just do it automatically when you wake up or go to bed.

Unhappiness is generally the result of our reality not meeting our expectations. To move toward happiness, we must begin by changing our mindset. We can bring unconscious money making decisions to the front of our minds. By examining these choices, we can ensure they are aligned with our goals. The first step to becoming conscious about our decisions starts with an understanding of what money means to us.

The Meaning of Money

What does money mean to you? Money can mean different things to different people. You might view it as a positive resource for achieving all that life has to offer. Or you might have a negative view of money, seeing it as the "root of all evil" that leads to greed and glut.

Money can be a source of inspiration and empowerment, or it can be a vehicle for your anxieties and fears. Much of our attitude toward money was formed when we were younger. As with most aspects of our personality, our parents can be a major influence on shaping who we become. This is especially true when it comes to the role that money plays in our lives.

You might have seen your parents struggle to pay their bills and put food on the table. Your dad might have worked two jobs, and your mom might have agonized over the mortgage. Maybe your parents fought a lot about money. Maybe you heard them blame politicians or talk about how the system's rigged. All these influences could instill a negative attitude toward money.

On the other hand, your parents might have embraced money as fuel for their lives. Maybe they were entrepreneurs or salespeople, where their income corresponded to how hard they worked. Maybe they experienced a financial hardship but figured out a way to move forward; they didn't blame anyone but took ownership of their problems. Perhaps they gave to charity and sought ways to serve their community. If you grew up in this household, you would have a different attitude toward money.

As you think back on your life, how did you learn about money? What role has money played in your life? One thing we know for sure is that you can't pick your parents. It's not your fault if you were raised with a negative attitude toward money. Yet, it is up to you to recognize and change it. Take the first step toward improving your money mindset by understanding your thoughts.

Fear Factor

As we go through life, our brains are hardwired to perceive dangers that could hurt or even kill us. Our amygdalae, the emotion center of the brain, pick up on these threats and cause a fight-or-flight response. For example, the hairs on the back of our neck stand up to warn us of impending threats, like the proverbial tiger rustling in the bushes. This fear factor can save us from impending doom or it can produce unwanted and unnecessary anxiety.

The need for our amygdalae has waned over the years. How many times has a tiger leaped out of the bushes at you? Rather than aiding our survival, the amygdale may overact and release fear chemicals that may cause us to act illogically.

As we use money in our lives, we might have similar feelings. Certain triggers may release a flood of these same chemicals, resulting in poor financial decision-making. A good example of this might be selling out of the stock market in the wake of a major news event. Panicking and acting while in this emotional state will cause you to deviate from your goals and move in the wrong direction.

Maybe your attitudes toward money run deeper than this. You might be someone who exhibits self-sabotaging behaviors that prevent you from ever realizing your goals. This could be because, on some level, you feel that you don't deserve it. You might be afraid of the new challenges that come with success.

Either way, try to bring these fears out into the open and examine them. Throughout the day, push back on your own limited thinking and remind yourself of the *why* that motivates you. Align your thoughts and actions with your purpose, and you will be on your way to creating the results that you want.

Feed Your Mind

Your mind is one of the most important parts of your body. Without it, you are not you. Just as you need to take care of your physical body through proper nutrition and exercise, so too does your mind need nourishment and care.

Your mind needs to be fed a variety of positive experiences and thoughts as much as you need to eat healthy and balanced meals. If you eat too many sweets, you may become overweight and unhealthy. Likewise, if you feed your mind too much junk, you'll dwell in fear and could become depressed.

Reframe each experience you have using a positive framework. Instead of saying that you *have* to go to work to earn a paycheck, you can focus on how lucky you are that you *get* to work and receive that paycheck. If you're stuck in a job you absolutely loathe, then focus on how you can use your current situation as a step in the direction of doing something that feels more fulfilling. Change your "have-to's" into "get-to's." This is the healthy sustenance that your mind needs to move your life in the right direction.

Use gratitude as a ritualistic practice to push out your negative programming and shine a bright light on the positives in your life. Your mind won't be able to process gratitude and fear at the same time. By training yourself to be grateful for all of life's experiences, you'll reprogram your mind to act from a place of confidence and purpose.

While it might seem corny at first, you'll notice how powerful this process can be. You might also consider using meditation or hypnosis techniques. These exercises speak directly to your subconscious mind, attacking the root of the problem head on. They can be quite relaxing too.

As a bonus for purchasing this book, download a free seven-minute money meditation at **www.bit.ly/fppbookbonus**.

You can also learn to focus your mind on abundance versus scarcity. There are trillions of dollars circulating in our economy and billions more are printed each year. Go to the Bureau of Printing and Engraving in Washington DC, and you'll marvel at how limitless money can be. Reject scarcity and choose to live a life of abundance. There's plenty of money for you to do everything you want and more.

Jim Rohn once said, "You are the average of the five people you spend the most time with." You might find that you're spending too much time around the wrong people. Misery loves company, and no good comes from swimming in the negative end of the pool. You're treading water and going nowhere when you undermine your positive efforts with negative influences.

You don't have to make a dramatic change and cut these people out of your life altogether. Choose to spend more time around positive people instead. Optimistic people will help motivate you, keep you disciplined, and influence your growth. In all likelihood, you'll have more fun as well.

Choose a couple people you admire and take them to lunch. You might be surprised to find that they have undergone similar experiences as you, yet they might be on the other side of the problem. Seek out their guidance in moving toward your goals while staying true to your purpose.

Keep in mind that even baby steps can move you in the right direction. Begin to reframe your mind and push out the negativity by taking one small action each day. Try and catch yourself before you revert to dwelling in fear.

Imagine if you told your child a scary bedtime story. Do you think they'll have trouble sleeping? Of course they will. You've programmed them with negative thoughts and emotions just before they enter the land of the subconscious, where their minds like to play around with ideas and thoughts.

Instead, we choose to tell our children happy bedtime stories that help them feel safe and empowered to take on the world. Consider doing the same for yourself. At the end of the day, reflect on what went well and what you hope to achieve in the near future.

Also, spend time thinking about three things that made you happy during the day. You might want to capture these notes in a journal. By writing these thoughts down, you're reinforcing the positivity in your mind. This will put you on the path toward achieving your dreams and goals.

Be kind to yourself and know that setbacks will happen. Take them in stride and persevere. Having a positive money mindset is a critical step to achieving financial freedom. You'll need it to appreciate financial success and the journey you took to achieve it.

Chapter 3
The Middle Class

I have spent my life judging the distance between
American reality and the American dream.
—*Bruce Springsteen*

The middle class in our country is, in a word, failing. With 76% of Americans living paycheck-to-paycheck and most people having little or no money in savings for emergencies, something is drastically askew. Our parents told us to keep our heads down, work hard, and save our money. At the same time, there's a definite disconnect between our actions and our desires.

The future, however, holds hope. By taking ownership of our finances, we can begin to dig ourselves out of the doldrums and create the life we desire. We can lift up the middle class and, together, achieve prosperity.

The Rise of the American Dream

James Truslow Adams, an American historian, popularized the term "the American dream." He defined the concept in his 1931 book *Epic America*. He stated that "life should be better and richer and fuller for everyone, with opportunity for each according to ability or achievement" regardless of social class or circumstances of birth. While our country has come a long way in furthering that vision, we have a lot more work to do.

America was founded as the "land of opportunity" for many immigrants who moved here to seek better lives for themselves and their families. They worked hard and pinched pennies to make ends meet. While much has changed in our country, Americans are still seeking ways to save money.

Adams' vision of the American dream mentions opportunities for everyone, but clearly, more opportunities await those who are on a higher socioeconomic rung. Not only is it hard to climb into the middle class and above, but it's also difficult to stay there.

So many forces out of our control threaten our financial position; the best course of action is preparation. Too many people believe that the likelihood a catastrophe would impact them is low enough to not consider it a realistic threat. That misconception leaves us highly vulnerable to the inevitable storms of life. This was evident during the financial crisis of 2008 when most of Americans were caught off guard by the housing market collapse and economic downturn. The ripple effects can still be felt today.

The threat doesn't always come in an obvious form. For example, you may be approached by an ailing family member who needs your help to pay for medications or caregivers. You may have a friend who's behind on their mortgage payments and needs just a little help to get back on track. Or you may have children who return home after college—the so-called "boomerang kids"—who need a place to live as they search for a job. Although being generous is a rewarding feeling, it can also set us back in achieving our financial goals.

People who give under these circumstances should be commended for their generosity and commitment to their values. Yet, they can avoid their own financial hardship if they prepare adequately. By planning for these situations in advance, you'll stay on track toward your own financial success.

With most Americans focused on the day-to-day, it's hard to see the bigger picture. Les Brown explained the problem with this when he said, "You can't see the picture if you're in the frame." We must challenge our thinking, gain perspective, and push ourselves to be more intentional.

A Land of Inequalities

Our country is made up of many different types of people; that's what makes it so great. But the results of these differences can be astounding. We face geographic, socioeconomic, and gender wage disparity. These challenges, as well as racial and civil unrest that's brewing underneath the surface, prove that our economic melting pot is boiling over.

Where we live makes a dramatic difference in what it takes for a family of four to pay their bills. The Family Budget Calculator on the Economic Policy Institute's website[3] makes this clear. Plug in any city in the US, and you'll see the average household budget. Let's consider two similar cities with contrasting financial situations.

Dallas, Texas. Home of the Cowboys and Southfork Ranch. The Dallas-Fort Worth Metroplex is home to 6.9 million people according to 2014 Census Data. It spans 9,300 square miles, which is larger than Rhode Island and Connecticut combined. According to the EPI Calculator, the average family of four needs to bring in $61,000 annually to make ends meet.

In contrast, the Washington DC Metro area has a population of about 5.9 million people, and it spans about 6,600 square miles. Using the same calculator, a family of four would need $106,500 per year to pay its bills. That's a little less than double the figure for the average Dallas-Fort Worth family. Here we have two bustling cities that are similar in size but with hugely different economic profiles.

---

[3] "Family Budget Calculator," Economic Policy Institute, accessed December 09, 2016, http://www.epi.org/resources/budget.

The median household income is about $58,000 in the Dallas-Fort Worth Metroplex and $90,500 in the DC Metro area.[4] That means that in both locations, many middle-class families are struggling to pay their bills. This theme carries over to dozens of areas throughout the country. It's certainly not the rosy picture of the American dream that we expected.

From a macro perspective, the middle class has been stuck in the same income-earning zone for the last 50 years, unlike the upper class. During the 1980s and 1990s, the top 20% of income earners in America saw a significant jump in their salaries. To make matters worse, since the Great Recession in 2008, the average American is actually earning less each year, not more (on an inflation-adjusted basis).[5] The rich get richer while the middle class stagnates.

Even though "the Joneses" are struggling to put food on the table, our country's workforce has evolved over the last 50 years. We've become more tolerant and accepting of women and minorities. According to the United States Census Bureau, in 1967, 28.8% (14.8 million) of the workforce was female. In 2009, that number jumped to 43.5% (43.2 million).[6]

This has made our country more productive and profitable. If you think of the US as a company, it's as if we went on a major hiring spree and doubled the number of productive employees, adding more value to the bottom line.

---

[4] Niche, accessed December 09, 2016, http://www.niche.com/.

[5] "The American Middle Class Is Losing Ground." Pew Research Center's Social & Demographic Trends Project. 2015. Accessed December 09, 2016, http://www.pewsocialtrends.org/2015/12/09/the-american-middle-class-is-losing-ground/.

[6] DeNavas-Walt, C., Richardson, M. E., & Stringfellow, M. A. (2010, September). "Income, Poverty, and Health Insurance Coverage in the United States: 2009."

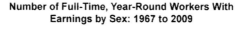

**Number of Full-Time, Year-Round Workers With
Earnings by Sex: 1967 to 2009**

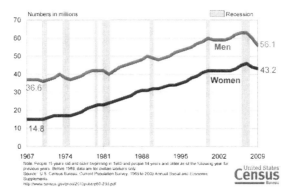

While progress has been made, we still have a lot more work to do. A woman is paid on average $0.79 for every dollar a man is paid. The pay gap is even worse for minority women. The American Association of University Women (AAUW) found that in 2014 Hispanic, African American, American Indian, and Native Hawaiian women had lower median annual earnings compared with non-Hispanic white and Asian American women.[7]

Most people point toward education to solve this problem. The more educated we are, the more we earn. While this might be true, it's a poor solution to the wage gap issue. It turns out that the more educated the woman, the greater the disparity in wages. The AAUW suggests women gain negotiation skills to help themselves out of this discrepancy.

A Hope for Our Future

The American dream is not dead; it's just harder to feel successful than it has ever been before. The middle class is falling behind, and most of us have major hurdles to overcome to achieve financial

---

[7] "The Simple Truth about the Gender Pay Gap (Fall 2016)." AAUW: Empowering Women Since 1881. Fall 2016. Accessed December 09, 2016, http://www.aauw.org/research/the-simple-truth-about-the-gender-pay-gap/.

prosperity. Yet as President Theodore Roosevelt said, "Nothing in the world is worth having or worth doing unless it means effort, pain, difficulty…"

Innovators like Elon Musk, Steve Jobs, and Jeff Bezos are this century's Edison, Ford, and Einstein. They've pushed the boundaries of our society, leading Americans to greater prosperity. But who will lead us individually?

We must empower ourselves to stay motivated to achieve our own financial goals. We need to take ownership of our finances and make smarter financial decisions. Focusing on education, discipline, and accountability, we become better leaders and advocates for ourselves. Putting it all together, we create our own financial freedom.

Part 2
Your Financial Pieces

Chapter 4
Cash Flow and Debt Management

The first time I had disposable income, the two things
I cared most about were a television and a couch.
—Seth Meyers

Cash is king. The more we have in our savings accounts, the more options we have in our lives. So, why do we limit ourselves by not having liquid reserves? According to a 2014 Bankrate.com survey, 62% of respondents have major cash challenges.[8] That translates to not being able to afford, for example, an unexpected emergency room visit or even a $500 car repair.

By not holding extra funds for a rainy day, we're taking on debt at a rapid rate. In 2016, the Federal Reserve found that 38.1% of households held credit card balances. That's down from 44% in 2009.[9] Even so, the average credit card balance per household has increased

---

[8] Claes Bell, CFA, "Budgeting Can Crumble In Times Of Trouble | Bankrate.com," January 7, 2015, accessed December 09, 2016, http://www.bankrate.com/finance/smart-spending/money-pulse-0115.aspx.

[9] "The 2014 Consumer Financial Literacy Survey - Nfcc.org," accessed December 9, 2016, https://www.nfcc.org/NewsRoom/FinancialLiteracy/files2013/NFCC_2014FinancialLiteracySurvey_datasheet_and_key_findings_031314%20FINAL.pdf.

to $5,700 or $16,048 for households carrying balances.[10]

With financial education becoming more mainstream, we still need more. As a country, why can't we seem to move ourselves forward? We feel that we can treat ourselves with a nice dinner out, drinks with friends, or even that luxury watch. After all, we work so hard that it's okay to splurge every once in a while, right? Unfortunately, those financial purchases are the reason why 76% of Americans live paycheck-to-paycheck.

If only we were conscious about our spending habits in the moment, day to day. A good balance of spending and saving will help you make progress toward your goals. This balance will provide you with the best of both worlds. It leaves room for fun purchases today while still moving you towards long-term prosperity.

Cash and Cash Flow

Whether you earn a steady salary or unpredictable commissions, your income is the lifeblood of your budget. To maintain a healthy budget, you must spend less than you earn. Any extra money left over is your discretionary income.

As a bonus for purchasing this book, download a short worksheet to create and organize your own budget at **www.bit.ly/fppbookbonus**.

You may decide to use your discretionary income to enhance your lifestyle. Maybe you'd like to go on a shopping spree, buy your friends a round of drinks, or even take that dream vacation. We need to understand that having discretionary income isn't the only ingredient to creating a successful financial future. It's knowing what to do with it that makes the difference between success and failure.

Consider paying yourself first by treating your monthly savings as a bill. You have to pay for utilities, food, and a mortgage or rent, why not pay your investment account as well? While we intend to save whatever's leftover, we often find a way to use that extra money for

---

[10] "Average Credit Card Debt in America: 2016 Facts & Figures," ValuePenguin, accessed December 09, 2016, https://www.valuepenguin.com/average-credit-card-debt.

other things. If we pay ourselves first, then we're making our financial future a priority.

As you pay your bills, determine the best way for you to manage and organize your finances. As long as you pay off the balance each month, using a credit card to pay for your expenses can be a good idea. Many cards provide rewards points for using their platform. They will also provide you instant feedback on how you're spending your money.

If you notice that you're tempted to carry a balance on your card, then this may not be the best tool for you. Instead, consider using a debit card. It will provide the same budget tracking without the need for cash.

Although few and far between, some places may not accept plastic, so keeping a bit of cash on you doesn't hurt. But stay aware of how often you're tapping the ATM. Don't forget to keep some checks on hand as well. Some vendors will only accept cash or check.

Money is a major point of contention for most married couples. Some couples hold separate bank accounts and credit cards and this can become quite cumbersome. Merging financial accounts can make managing your budget easier. Either way, find a system that works for you.

As with anything in a successful marriage, being open and honest is key. This is especially true when it comes to your financial habits and personal spending. Open communication will create a united front when trying to achieve your joint financial goals.

As you decide on a bank for your working accounts, find one that fits your unique situation. Consider using a checking account for your inflows and outflows. Also, open a savings account for emergency reserves and saving for short-term goals.

Experts usually recommend between three and six months' worth of expenses stashed away for a rainy day. If your job is fairly secure and you earn a consistent salary, you might opt for three months of reserves. If you have variable income or if your job is in jeopardy, you might want to set aside a six-month cushion.

If you don't mind a two-day delay in accessing your money, consider an online direct savings account. They can usually offer a higher interest rate since they don't have the overhead of a brick and mortar branch. Most are still insured by the Federal Deposit Insurance Corporation (FDIC) like other banks.

It makes sense to use bank savings accounts for any goal where you need principal protection. The time horizon for short-term savings goals is generally less than three to five years. A common example is a house or car down payment. Choosing to invest these funds could put your money at risk so that you might not have a sufficient amount available when you need it.

Debt Management

Debt doesn't ruin financial situations; people ruin financial situations. Debt carries a large emotional and financial burden, yet not all debt is bad. In some cases, debt can have a major negative impact on a financial plan. When used strategically, debt can have the opposite effect.

Are you using the debt to help improve your situation or as a crutch for a bad financial habit? Taking out a loan to buy a house is generally not a bad use of debt. You're buying a piece of real estate that has value and creating a place for you and your family to call home.

What about student loans? There's no question that our country's young people are saddled with monstrous amounts of student loan payments. This can be quite overwhelming for individuals just starting out in their careers and presumably in the lowest income earning years of their lives.

Those with large amounts of debt may even feel as if they are being held hostage by their banks. There might be a sense that they can't move their lives forward without getting rid of the monkey on their backs. While education debt can be quite oppressive at times, we forget what life would be like without a college degree at all.

Without the debt, you may not have been able to afford college at all. This normally results in earning a lower salary than you otherwise would. In a 2013 Pew Research Study, diploma-holding millennials had annual incomes $17,500 greater than those without a college degree.[11]

Adding it up, you will earn about $700,000 more over your career than if you had decided not to attend college at all. This doesn't account for raises or bonuses along the way too. Framing it like this makes taking on that debt a great investment. The same exercise could be done with graduate school and other advanced degrees as well.

Sometimes, taking on student debt may not make much financial sense. Maybe you want to go back to school, but your career won't provide any extra compensation for the added education. In situations like these, you'll have to weigh the emotional desire to further your education against the added expense you'll be incurring.

Not only does debt have a role in building education, but also in helping to grow a business. Almost one million new businesses are created each year in our country. Many businesses begin as a dream or an idea. They can never reach their full potential unless the economics of the business work out. It takes working capital to lay the framework for new products and innovations to come to the market. Being able to borrow money can be a blessing for that small business owner who needs just a little help getting their idea off the ground.

Using debt strategically might be a good way to enhance your financial position. At the same time, you will owe interest for that privilege. As you begin to pay back your debt, create a payment strategy that sorts each credit line by interest rate. Pay off the debt with the highest interest rate first. This will ensure that you're paying the least amount of interest.

Consider comparing the net interest rates of the debt lines as well. Some debt is tax deductible, and the net interest rate is the true rate that you'll be paying after the tax savings. For example, if you have a

---

[11] "The Rising Cost of Not Going to College," Pew Research Center's Social & Demographic Trends Project, 2014, accessed December 09, 2016, http://www.pewsocialtrends.org/2014/02/11/the-rising-cost-of-not-going-to-college/.

4% mortgage rate and you're in the 25% tax bracket, then your net interest rate is 3%.[12] Keep in mind that while mortgage debt can be tax deductible, it is subject to phase limitations. If you make too much money, you may begin to lose this tax benefit.

Making Financial Decisions

We've all heard it before: Cut that expensive latte habit or brown-bag your lunch, and it will make a big difference. By cutting out a small expensive habit, you can free up extra funds to grow into the future.

Let's take a look at how a hypothetical person, Patty, can build wealth by just eliminating her $6 latte habit and brewing coffee at home. After accounting for the cost of a coffee machine, grinder, and beans, Patty would be able to save $5 per day. Over the course of a year, that adds up to a total annual amount of $1,825.

Patty wants to know how much she can put away for retirement if she saves that $5 beginning when she is 25 years old and continuing for 40 years. She projects that she could potentially earn an annualized rate of 8% during this time. In doing the calculation, Patty figures that she would have saved about $500,000.

One thing Patty forgot to factor into this calculation is inflation. Inflation measures how much prices rise over time. It's a consequence of a growing economy. Some inflation is good. Too much or too little causes concern.

That $5 cup of joe will most likely increase in price over 40 years— let's say about 2% each year. Once Patty reaches 65 years old, it may cost a little less than $11 for that same coffee. If she invested the cost of that coffee each year, she'd have about $640,000.

Now, that $640,000 won't be worth as much as it is today due to our friend inflation. Considering she changed only one small habit, that's still pretty decent. While this can be a powerful savings tactic, it should not discourage you from splurging every once in a while. Life's too short for us not to enjoy it. If that expensive latte is your treat for

---

[12] 4% x (100% - 25%) = 3%

yourself that brings you joy and energy, then find somewhere else to trim.

The decision to brew her own coffee didn't just save Patty $5 today, but a lot more than that over her lifetime. This is called opportunity cost. The loss or gain between two alternatives should be weighed against each other.

For example, let's look at Tom who decides to quit working and go back to school for further training. The cost of his decision isn't only the cost of the tuition. It's also the opportunity cost of his lost wages for the year he's in school.

As Tom is trying to decide if this decision makes sense, he needs to consider his future earnings as well. The increase in his income would need to offset the cost of the year of school plus the year of salary that he gave up. This is an important concept to consider, as it applies to a variety of areas of life. We often make decisions without considering opportunity cost and what we're giving up.

Other times, we make financial decisions based too much on what happened in the past. Sunk costs are those that we've already paid that cannot be recovered. Take Julie for example. She bought tickets to a rock concert two months ago. It turns out her friends are getting together that same night to play board games. Even though Julie would rather hang out with her friends, she decides to go to the rock concert anyways. She has already spent the money on the tickets and doesn't want them to go to waste.

Sunk costs also apply in the stock market. Michael buys $2,500 worth of XYZ stock. The company falls on hard times, and his shares are now worth only $1,500. Michael holds on to the shares because he invested $2,500 and doesn't want to take a loss. His decision to hold the shares shouldn't be based on what he paid for the shares, however. It should be based on his expectation of how the company will perform in the future. It's hard for us to cut our losses because we want to make our investments worthwhile. We also don't want to appear foolish for making the wrong decision.

Sunk costs go hand in hand with the concept of loss aversion. As humans, we tend to prefer avoiding losses over securing gains. Most studies suggest that losses pack twice as much psychological potency as gains. That's why we sell out of a declining stock market and have trouble getting back in while it increases. We'd rather sit on the sidelines, missing the upswing than to be in it and risk experiencing the loss again. We'll look at an example that illustrates this point further in the next chapter.

Making investment choices based on these decision-making traps can be challenging. They can bruise both our egos and our portfolio returns. Ultimately, they move us away from our financial goals and place us further behind.

Chapter 5
Investment Strategies

*We simply attempt to be fearful when others are greedy
and to be greedy only when others are fearful.*
—Warren Buffett

Now that we've designed a strategy to manage our cash flow and debts, it's time to consider investing. Many people jump right into investing without examining their current financial position first. Just as you can't play basketball on a court full of quicksand, you need solid financial footing to invest.

Risk is inherent in the investment world. You'll want to consider how much risk you're willing to take and align your investment selection with your risk profile. Also, use fundamental investment techniques to minimize your risk and maximize your potential return.

The Hot Stock Tip

Where do most people get their investing tips? If you're like most people, then you've probably received some unsolicited advice from a friend or family member to buy a hot stock. While your friend might have made tons of money from their investment skills, many times jumping into an investment opportunity after it has already gone up, may not be prudent. Let's review an example.

You meet your friend George for coffee, and he tells you about this great stock that has done nothing but go up. He bought in at $20 per share, and it's now worth $36. So, you decide to sign up for an online brokerage account and buy 100 shares.

After a couple of days, you look at your account. The stock is now worth $40 per share. You get excited and thank your friend for his advice. A week later, you look at your account. The stock's now hovering at $37 per share, and you've lost almost all of your gains. No problem, at least you're still up. You check it again a couple weeks later and realize that the share price is down to $33 per share. You start to get nervous but hang in there. Since you're worried about it, you start logging into your account daily to watch the stock.

Over the next few days, the stock continues to drop and finishes out the week at $24.50. You think long and hard about it over the weekend and decide that if the stock drops to $20, you're going to cut your losses. By Wednesday of the next week it fulfills your negative expectation and you sell. Then you call up your friend to give him a piece of your mind.

This scenario plays out time and time again. In fact, many sitcoms devote an entire episode surrounding this plotline. Your friend's intentions were good; however, what works for him might not work for you. Timing is everything, and if you're speculating in the stock market, then you must understand what is actually going on there.

In a free market, for every buyer there's a seller. When you are buying at $36 per share, institutional money managers are selling out and taking profits. When you sell out at $20 per share, those same institutional managers are buying back in, seeing great value in the share price.

While you can get lucky occasionally and pick some winners, it's impossible to time the market exactly right. Institutional investors aren't watching their stock positions daily and have sophisticated models that take emotion out of the equation. Warren Buffett, one of the greatest investors of our time, speaks to this as part of his contrarian investment philosophy. He says, "We simply attempt to be fearful when others are greedy and to be greedy only when others are fearful."

Portfolio Design

Taking emotions out of investing is one of the hardest things to do. You've worked so hard to build your nest egg, and you want to ensure it doesn't vanish into thin air. That's why it's important to take a snapshot of your risk tolerance every few years to figure out how much you are willing to give up for the possibility of gains.

Once you've established a baseline for your risk appetite, the next—and most forgettable—step is to select an investment allocation to reflect your investment profile. Many people see stocks as risky and bonds as safe; however, that's not always true. You can choose stocks that are, relatively speaking, safe, and you can find risky bonds as well.

Digging deeper into building out your portfolio, you'll want to pick a variety of types of stocks and bonds to make up your allocation. According to Harry Markowitz's Modern Portfolio Theory [13], diversifying your investment mix across many non-correlated asset classes will potentially increase your expected returns while minimizing risk. The important thing to note is that you want the asset classes to be non-correlated, or unrelated to each other. This will give you a diversity of investment options that act differently in different market scenarios.

If the stock market drops, you'd want a portion of your portfolio to be stable or potentially even to grow in that environment. Certain types of investments aren't tied to how the stock market performs. Some examples are real estate, commodities, and natural resources. Although these types of investments alone would heighten your level of risk, adding small quantities of them to a diversified portfolio may lower a portfolio's overall risk and potentially increase the return.

---

[13] Harry Markowitz, "Portfolio Selection," *Journal of Finance*, 1952.

Your goal isn't to pick the winning category every time but to invest in all categories with either a goal of long-term growth or protection of principal. Diversification is a method used to manage risk. It doesn't guarantee investment returns or eliminate the risk of loss.

One common mistake individuals make when creating portfolios is not selecting an optimal mix of investment categories. By building an efficient portfolio, you may be able to lower your risk and enhance your return. This is where hiring an investment advisor can help to maximize your portfolio's potential.

As a bonus for purchasing this book, you can download a sample risk tolerance quiz and the corresponding model portfolios at **www.bit.ly/fppbookbonus**.

Account Types

To begin your investment journey, you'll need to open an account at a brokerage house or with an investment advisor. The type of account you open will greatly depend on what you intend to do with the money. If you have a long-term goal, like saving for retirement, you might choose to open an Individual Retirement Account (IRA). If you have a mid-term goal, like saving for a house down payment and would like to access your funds before you hit retirement age, then you might consider a non-qualified brokerage account. If you're a minor, then you'll need to open a custodial account with a guardian.

- **Retirement Accounts**

Each account type carries with it a certain set of tax rules. IRAs are the most common type of individually-owned retirement accounts. A 401(k) is like the IRA's cousin held by an employer and regulated under a slightly different set of rules. Both IRAs and 401(k)s come in either "Traditional" or "Roth" flavors.

Traditional accounts can accept pretax contributions and defer the tax on the growth into the future. When the money is taken out in retirement, the full withdrawal is taxable at your ordinary income tax rate at that time. With Roth accounts, money is invested using after-tax dollars. Growth on the investment is tax-deferred, and in retirement, the entire account balance can be withdrawn tax-free.

If funds are withdrawn before the age of 59 ½, there's generally a 10% penalty assessed. Tax benefits on IRAs are subject to income limits, depending on your situation, so be sure to review the appropriate thresholds before you invest.

As of 2010, the government allows you to convert your traditional IRA to a Roth IRA without a penalty. You must pay the taxes on the amount converted. This can be a key opportunity if you desire tax favorable withdrawals.

An investors' anticipated tax bracket in retirement will determine whether a Roth or traditional IRA would make more sense. Generally, investors who believe they will pay lower tax rates in retirement might not benefit as much from this strategy. Even still, each situation is unique and should be evaluated based on the specific circumstances.

- **Brokerage Accounts**

If you plan on withdrawing your investment before you retire, you might consider opening a non-qualified brokerage account. With these accounts, you forgo some of the tax benefits that retirement accounts boast in exchange for the ability to access the funds before retirement without penalty.

As your investment grows, you may end up owing taxes along the way. You may qualify for capital gains tax rates on some of the money too. This is a tax on any gains you've made in your investment and can sometimes qualify for a lower rate.

Keep good records of your cost basis for your investments. Cost basis is the amount you paid for the shares that you own, plus any dividends or capital gains that were reinvested. This will help when it comes time to sell your shares and determine the capital gains taxes that you owe.

- ## Custodial Accounts

Custodial accounts are those opened by a guardian on behalf of a minor. They are taxed under "kiddie tax" rules, where some investment income is tax-free, some taxed at the child's rate, and the remainder at the parent's rate. The thresholds for these tax brackets are usually indexed for inflation, so be sure to review them each year.

The kiddie tax rule was created to prevent parents from using their children's accounts as a tax shelter. Even with the limitations, custodial accounts are great starter accounts for minors and can be used for teaching kids about money.

After you've selected the right type of account for you, you'll need to decide how to invest the money. Within each of these accounts, you can hold a variety of different investment instruments. Think of the account type as the mode of transportation and the investment instrument as you and your luggage. You'd fit nicely in a car, plane, train, or boat, and if used appropriately, each can be economical and get you to where you want to go.

Investment Instruments

There are a variety of ways to invest in the markets. Most people want to go straight to investing in their favorite stocks. Certainly, buying 100 shares of your favorite stock can be a fun way to get started as a new investor. Yet, when it comes to creating a portfolio with less volatility potential, that is more stability, using broader-based investment instruments, like mutual funds and Exchange traded funds (ETFs), tend to be more practical.

A mutual fund is a broad-based pool of investments, usually managed by a tenured money manager. The manager and team are responsible for selecting the right mix of stocks, bonds, or some combination that align with the mandated fund objective. Some mutual funds target a specific category of instruments, like stock in large or international companies. Others might be diversified investments in themselves. A common example of this is a target-date fund.

Target-date funds create a mixture of investments based on your targeted retirement date. For example, a target-date 2040 fund is a basket of investments that becomes more conservative as the year 2040 approaches. These are great tools to use for small accounts since they make investing easy. Keep in mind that any money invested in these funds is not guaranteed at any time. This includes any investments at or after the fund's specific target retirement date.

Once your account grows to over $25,000 or $50,000, creating your own portfolio mix might save you in fees and allow you to customize your portfolio for your own specific risk tolerance and overall investment strategy. Additionally, target-date funds may miss some investment categories that could comprise an optimal portfolio, like real estate, natural resources, or international bonds.

Each mutual fund charges an investment management fee, which goes toward paying for the money manager and their team. These fees can be found in the fund's prospectus, which your financial advisor must provide. Some funds charge additional fees, called sales charges, which go to the advisor who sold the funds to you.

If you are in an investment advisory relationship, however, the advisor charges a management fee instead and generally waives the sales load and other investment fees. Investment advisory accounts provide a platform for you and your advisor to work together to manage your portfolio on an ongoing basis.

One other note about mutual funds is the tax implications of holding them. If you purchase a mutual fund outside of a tax-qualified account, like a 401(k) or IRA, then you might be in for a rude awakening come tax time. Since mutual funds buy and sell investments throughout the year, they themselves are generating taxable gains and losses.

Once a year, they are required to distribute those gains to you in addition to any dividends disclosed. While you personally may not have sold out of the fund, you will have to recognize the capital gain distribution on your tax return. Many mutual funds wait until the end of the year to distribute their capital gains, so watch the timing of when you buy into these investment instruments.

While the biggest benefit of investing in mutual funds is diversification, there are some drawbacks. As a result of these challenges, the industry created an investment tool that addresses many of these issues while still providing a way for individual investors to diversify their investments.

Exchange traded funds, or ETFs, have features similar to both mutual funds and stocks. They are similar to mutual funds in that they are pooled funds that diversify the underlying investments and usually track a predetermined index, like the S&P 500. The S&P 500 is an unmanaged index comprised of the top 500 companies in America and a widely accepted gauge of the market as a whole.

ETFs are similar to stocks in that ETFs are bought and sold throughout the day as opposed to settling at the end of the day. They usually are not actively managed and therefore have dramatically lower management fees. They may also be more tax efficient since there is little buying and selling of the underlying investment portfolio.

Mutual funds and ETFs are sold by prospectus. As previously mentioned, these prospectuses outline the investment objectives, risks, fees, charges, and expenses. You should read and consider this information carefully before investing. Investments will fluctuate and, when redeemed, may be worth more or less than when originally invested. ETFs hold the same risks as direct stock ownership. ETFs structured as "fund of funds" will entail the same risks associated with the underlying funds.

Many people in the investment world debate whether it's better to hire a mutual fund manager to actively manage your money or to just simply invest passively in an index. It's said that it is nearly impossible to beat the market on a consistent basis. Why spend the fees for active management trying to *beat* the market when you can buy index funds that attempt to *be* the market? Others argue that selecting a few good quality money managers can provide an added level of benefit to the portfolio.

This is where an investment advisor can help you create a portfolio that addresses to your individual needs and preferences to find the optimal mix of active and passive management. In some investment categories, active management might hold a distinct advantage. However, in other categories replicating the category benchmark with a passive management style might prove better.

Timing the Market

As we get ready to invest, we tend to question whether it's the right time. We think that with so much uncertainty and volatility, maybe it's best to wait until the dust settles. The truth is the right time to invest is whenever you're ready. Nobody has a crystal ball to predict what's going to happen next, and often our emotions can mislead us.

If you think you do possess the skillset to predict market patterns, consider the implications of getting it wrong. By missing out on the 10 most profitable trading days of the S&P 500 Index over the 20-year period from 1995–2014, you would have decreased your average annual performance by almost 4%.[14] On an initial investment of $10,000, that mistake could cost you $32,788 in investment returns.

If you think you know when the best and worst days were, think again because you're probably wrong. Six of those top 10 days actually occurred within two weeks of the 10 worst trading days. This means that if you had gone on vacation or had a family emergency that took

---

[14] J.P. Morgan Asset Management using data from Lipper. 20-year annualized returns are based on the S&P 500 Total Return Index, an unmanaged, capitalization weighted index that measures the performance of 500 large capitalization domestic stocks representing all major industries. Past performance is not indicative of future returns. An individual cannot invest directly in an index. Data is from December 31,2014.

you away from your portfolio for a few days, you could have missed out on some major returns.

Bouncing in and out of the market can dramatically impact your financial goals and erode returns on investments over the long run. While this is generally not a recommended strategy to take, there are some other approaches to consider that address the risk that you're investing at the wrong time.

• Dollar-Cost Averaging

With dollar-cost averaging, an investor is taking their money and dividing it up into periodic payments into the market. For example, Sarah wants to invest $60,000 into the market. Instead of investing all $60,000 in a lump sum, she might consider investing $5,000 per month for 12 months. This would allow Sarah to buy into the market at a variety of different levels and alleviate any worry that she mistimed her investment.

During the time she is dollar-cost averaging, Sarah would actually want the market to drop because she would acquire more shares with the same $5,000. The theory behind this strategy relates to the grocery shopper who has a $10 budget each week to spend on pasta. When pasta is $1 per box, she can purchase 10 boxes, but when pasta is on sale for $0.50 per box, she can buy 20 boxes for the same $10. As shown by this example, dollar-cost averaging helps take the guesswork out of the market, with a consistent investment approach that allows you to buy more shares of stock at lower prices and less shares at higher prices.

Dollar-cost averaging doesn't guarantee a profit and doesn't protect against loss in declining markets. Additionally, since such a program involves regular investment purchases regardless of fluctuating price levels of the investment, you should consider your financial ability to continue purchases through periods of low price levels.

- **Rebalancing**

Another strategy to employ to decrease your risk exposure is to rebalance your portfolio. As markets ebb and flow, your original investment mix might become out of balance with your specific model portfolio. Rebalancing takes the categories where you may be overvalued and moves them to those segments that are undervalued.

For example, your investment objective might be to hold 60% of your money in stock-based investments and 40% in bond-based ones. If the stock market (and your stocks in particular) did exceptionally well one year, your stock-based investments might become a larger percentage of the whole, say 68%. As time goes on, your portfolio can shift dramatically out of balance, exposing the portfolio to greater risk. Your goal here is to maintain a portfolio in line with your risk tolerance.

As you apply this strategy you might feel hesitant as you will be consistently selling out of the investments that are doing well and buying into those that might be doing less well by comparison. Resist the temptation to reject this strategy since systematically rebalancing will help you keep your emotions out of it.

Typically, you should rebalance your portfolio at least twice a year. It's also a good idea to meet with an investment advisor regularly. You don't want to hover over your portfolio, but you don't want to forget about it either.

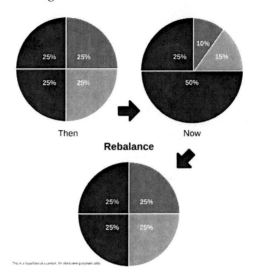

Then   Now

Rebalance

Benchmarking

As you create a diversified portfolio, you may tend to compare your investment returns with the overall performance of the stock market—or worse, have no basis for comparison at all. Investors commonly refer to the S&P 500 Index as a way to benchmark their performance. While this seems logical, it can lead to a great deal of confusion. For one thing, you cannot invest directly in an index.

Since you are breaking your portfolio into many different categories, only a small portion of your portfolio should be invested in instruments comparable to the large companies found in the S&P 500 index. You may have other stock-based categories, like small companies, internationals, and real estate. In addition, you could have domestic and international bonds in your portfolio. As you review your portfolio, you'll want to match each category that you're invested in with its corresponding index.

Let's take an overly simplistic example to understand how to benchmark your portfolio's performance in reality. If your portfolio is invested 50% in large company stocks and 50% in domestic bonds, then you would benchmark your stock portion against the S&P 500

Index and the bond portion against the Barclays U.S. Aggregate Bond Index.[15]

As you build out more asset classes in your portfolio, you'll want to add more indexes to your benchmark. For example, for your international stocks, you'll want to use an international equity index. After doing this for each asset class, you'll have a benchmark that fits your portfolio's unique makeup and will be a way to evaluate your performance.

Benchmarking your portfolio this way would be the technical way to evaluate your performance. You may choose to abandon this methodology and go straight to a goals-based evaluation. By choosing to review your portfolio as it relates to your goals, it will help you keep the market volatility in perspective while staying focused on a 30,000-foot view of how things are progressing.

For example, your portfolio may be intended for a retirement savings goal. If your goal is to have $1 million in your account by age 65, you'll want to evaluate how you're progressing toward that goal. If your portfolio balance is $500,000, then you'll know that you're halfway to goal. As the portfolio goes up and down, you'll spend more time on what matters most—the goal of retiring at 65—and less time on the monotony of rates of return.

As you create your investment plan, you'll have created a strategy designed to enhance investment returns and reduce risk, all while staying focused on your desired financial goals. You'll also want to be mindful of some of the adverse investor behavior that could impede your growth or even cause you to lock in losses. In the end, the goal is to be confident with your investments and know they are working for you with a plan in place to help you achieve your financial goals and ultimately financial freedom.

---

[15] The Barclays US Aggregate Bond Index is a broad-based bond index comprised of government, corporate, mortgage, and asset-backed issues, rated investment grade or higher, and having at least one year to maturity.

Chapter 6
Retirement Planning

When I finally retire, I just want to go away so no one has to listen to me.
—Steve Martin

Retirement means different things to different people. Some people would love to quit their day job today and travel the world. Others might want to scale back their hours and ease into a more moderate-paced lifestyle. Some might even take up a second career or start a small business. Whatever your vision is for retirement, proper planning will help you achieve financial independence.

Many of us don't plan appropriately for retirement, one of the biggest lifestyle changes of our lives. According to the Economic Policy Institute's report "The State of American Retirement,"[16] about half of American households have no retirement savings at all. What's worse is that the median IRA account balance for someone in their early 50s is a mere $31,692 and only $55,807 in their early 60s,

---

[16] "The State of American Retirement: How 401(k)s Have Failed Most American Workers," Economic Policy Institute, accessed December 09, 2016, http://www.epi.org/publication/retirement-in-america/.

according to the Employee Benefit Research Institute.[17] This is not nearly enough to create an income stream to sustain 30–40 years of expenses, especially with the expectation of inflation.

Managing your portfolio during the accumulation phase of your life differs from managing during the distribution phase. Retirees most fear outliving their assets and being forced to return to work. A quality retirement income plan will speak to your specific goals, as well as provide a sense of security that your lifestyle will be sustainable.

This Retirement Life

Your retirement lifestyle might be less than, equal to, or even greater than your current one. Using rule-of-thumb methods may backfire, as they don't speak to your specific situation, and some are even outdated.

To create your retirement plan, first envision what your life will look like during your golden years. Many people wait their entire lives for this phase of life. You might have deferred certain activities or hobbies until retirement. Use your time wisely; you've earned it.

Most retirees experience retirement in three phases, all of which blend together over the passage of time. Let's review these three phases.

• The Dawn Phase

The Dawn Phase is the initial retirement phase, between your mid-50s and early 60s. It may include the last couple years of your career and the first few years of your retirement transition. This period tends to involve gathering information to help you make informed financial decisions. You may be eager to run retirement projections to understand how long your money will last. These simulations can provide confidence that you will not outlive your money.

---

[17] Craig Copeland, Ph.D., "Individual Retirement Account Balances, Contributions, and Rollovers, 2013; With Longitudinal Results 2010–2013: The EBRI IRA Database," Employee Benefit Research Institute, May 2015, accessed December 9, 2016.

You might also be psychologically coming to terms with embarking on the last part of your life. Many people struggle with letting go of their careers or not going to work every day. Their careers might define who they think they are and give them a purpose to get out of bed. It's important to go easy on yourself during this phase. Build daily routines and structure so you won't develop the "retirement blues."

During this phase, you may also decide to downsize from your current home. You might choose a more sensible place to live with less space to maintain. Many retirees seek out 55+ communities to be around other retirees. You may also decide to become a snowbird and own multiple homes in different locations.

During the Dawn Phase, you might consider dialing down the risk for your retirement portfolio. You'll begin to use strategies to protect your nest egg. You might also consider paying down debt. Assuming you're going to stay in your home, consider paying off your mortgage. That's one less bill you'll have to pay and less retirement income you'll need.

Finally, you may decide to solidify what you will be doing with your new found free time. You might set aside more time for your favorite hobby. Maybe you want to take up a second career or travel and spend more time with family and friends. The Dawn Phase is all about formulating your strategy, making important lifestyle decisions, and preparing for a successful retirement.

- **The High Noon Phase**

The High Noon Phase relates to your mid-retirement years, between your early 60s and early 70s. This is when you are living the life that you've envisioned all these years. You actively pursue the items on your bucket list. You may still be working in some capacity. You might choose to consult for a bit, start a new business venture, or volunteer in some way. Whatever the situation, you'll be keeping your mind fresh without the stresses of the nine-to-five grind.

During this phase, you'll continue to examine your spending habits. You want to ensure that your budget estimates are accurate. If not, you may need to make some changes to the plan. You will also retool your investment portfolio to reflect your need for income.

Sometime during this period you'll reach 70 ½. This is the age when you'll take required distributions from your retirement accounts. Remember, just because you must withdraw the money from these accounts doesn't mean you have to spend it. Consider reinvesting extra funds if you are living well below your means. The High Noon Phase is all about enjoying life, having fun experiences, *and* maintaining financial stability.

- **The Dusk Phase**

The Dusk Phase begins around your early to mid-70s. This is the time when you will likely start to settle down. You may still travel a bit, but not at the same pace as you were. Managing your health might also grow in importance.

Also during this stage, your family may play a greater role in your life. This is the time to discuss how you'd like to participate in your family's financial plan. For example, you may implement a gifting strategy to help your grandkids pay for college.

It's critical to review your final documents to ensure they embody your current wishes. Be sure to review your full estate plan. This includes your will, advanced medical directives, and powers of attorney. The Dusk Phase centers on managing your health, reviewing the impact of your legacy, and spending your time in a meaningful way.

Keep in mind that each of us moves through these phases at our own pace. Your timeline may differ, but you should experience each phase at some point. Your retirement success directly correlates with the planning work that you've completed. During this stage, a financial planner continues to add value to the process. They can provide insights and help you keep your plan on track.

The Three-Legged Stool Has Fallen

Back in the good old days, you would work for a company for your entire career. In return for that loyalty, you'd receive a gold watch and a guaranteed income stream for the rest of your life. With your pension income, personal savings, and Social Security income, you'd be set. This was deemed the three-legged stool, as in the three sources of retirement income.

Unfortunately, the economic climate has changed. With only 26% of companies offering traditional pension plans,[18] it's becoming more challenging to create a secure source of retirement income. That means personal savings must play a more significant role in helping fuel your financial strategy for retirement. By letting employees take the investment risk and control their own retirement contributions, companies have lowered their costs and liability.

As a result, employees feel less loyal to the companies they work for. According to the Bureau of Labor Statistics, the average American worker will hold 11.7 jobs between the ages of 18 and 48.[19] While companies have saved money by removing their pension plans, turnover costs have skyrocketed.

As the pension leg of the stool is knocked down, Americans will need to replace this income stream. Because Social Security isn't the answer, we'll need to rely on our personal savings. Unfortunately, we're not saving as much as we should. To replace a traditional pension, a 25-year-old would need to save about $1,250 per month for 40 years. This would provide an income stream of 50% of an annual salary of $75,000 at age 65. This is well beyond what many Americans can afford.

If you're one of the lucky workers with a pension, consider the different payout options. Providers usually offer either a straight life or joint and survivor option.

---

[18] *LIMRA The Retirement Income Reference Book*, 2012 ed.

[19] "Number of Jobs Held, Labor Market Activity, and Earnings Growth Among the Youngest Baby Boomers: Results from a Longitudinal Survey Summary," U.S. Bureau of Labor Statistics, 2015, accessed December 09, 2016, http://www.bls.gov/news.release/nlsoy.nr0.htm.

The straight life calculation will pay out the largest amount, but only for your lifetime. If you die the day after you select this option, then nothing passes to your spouse or children. A period certain provision can protect against this possibility because it guarantees a payout for a certain number of years, usually 10. While this provides more value, it comes with a price—a lower annuity payout.

The joint and survivor annuity feature protects your spouse if you pass away first. Typically, this is the most expensive option and will reduce your income stream the most. Additionally, this feature usually pays only to a spouse, so if you both pass away at the same time, then no residual benefits go to other beneficiaries.

One strategy that can help defray some of these costs is combining permanent life insurance and a straight life pension. Instead of buying life insurance with a joint and survivor annuity, purchase a policy with a private insurer.

This strategy will only work if you are insurable. It also helps to be in good health and a nonsmoker so you can qualify for preferred health. By combining these two products, you can select the highest pension option while still protecting your heirs.

Federal Employee Retirement System (FERS)

Government employees are one of the last groups of people that still receive pension benefits. These defined benefit programs provide retirees a guaranteed income stream above and beyond any Social Security benefits and savings accumulated in retirement accounts. The FERS basic annuity formula depends on how old you are and how many service years you have when you retire.

Retire at 62 or older with 20 or more service years
"High-3" average pay x Number of Service Years x 1.1%

Retire under 62 OR 62 or older with less than 20 service years
"High-3" average pay x Number of Service Years x 1.0%

Social Security

Whether you have a pension or not, most people consider Social Security their defined income source for retirement. At the same time, concerns about the sustainability of the program have grown. If you're close to retirement, you probably have two major questions regarding Social Security. The first, "Will it be there for me?" and the second, "What's the best age to start taking benefits?"

The challenges facing the Social Security system are rooted in its past. Created in 1935, the system works on a pay-as-you-go basis. Taxes collected from today's workers pay for current retirees' benefits. As long as the money paid in remains greater than the money paid out, the system works.

But times have changed, and people now live longer than they did at the program's inception. In fact, when the Social Security program was enacted in 1935, the average life expectancy was 61 years old.[20] Today, the average life expectancy in the US is 79 years old.[21]

As a result, experts estimate that by 2021 more people will be collecting Social Security benefits than will be paying into the system. The Social Security Trust Fund, a reserve fund, will then be needed to support the benefits. By the mid-2030s, the Trust Fund will be exhausted. Experts estimate that only 77% of benefits will be covered by incoming payments.[22] Unless the system undergoes a dramatic overhaul to address the new demographic environment, we will have these major challenges in the future.

To address the uncertain direction of Social Security, it is a prudent strategy to adjust your income projections in your financial plan. If you're already close to your full retirement age, you'll likely receive benefits. Those who are further away should use more conservative assumptions about Social Security in your retirement plan. For some,

---

[20] Centers for Disease Control and Prevention, 2016, accessed December 09, 2016, http://www.cdc.gov/nchs/index.htm.
21 World Health Statistics 2016: Monitoring Health for the SDGs Sustainable Development Goals (World Health Organization, 2016).
[22] "Social Security," Trustees Report Summary, accessed December 09, 2016, https://www.ssa.gov/oact/trsum/.

estimating half of the projected benefit might be a good strategy. Others should eliminate the program entirely so that any income received from the system will exceed expectations.

The second question frequently asked about Social Security is when to begin receiving benefits. You have the option to claim your benefits any time after age 62, assuming you've earned enough credits to qualify. However, claiming Social Security early will reduce your benefits significantly. For example, if benefits are taken as early as possible, which currently is at age 62, you lose 30%. The amount of the reduction shrinks as you get closer to your full retirement age.

Also, if you claim Social Security at 62 and still plan on working, you'll need to watch for an earned income offset. For every $2 of income you earn beyond a certain threshold, your Social Security benefits are reduced by $1. Once you reach full retirement age, you can receive benefits with no limits on earnings.

You have the option of waiting to claim benefits beyond your full retirement age. Your benefits could increase by as much as 8% every year you wait between full retirement age and 70. After you reach age 70, you derive no additional benefit for waiting.

Deciding when to claim your Social Security benefits is a personal choice. Many experts recommend waiting as long as possible to take advantage of higher income payouts. The best time to claim your benefits depends on factors such as your health, marital status, other income sources, and life expectancy. Your financial advisor can offer you an independent perspective based on your circumstances and discuss how Social Security benefits fit within your overall retirement plan.

When putting a retirement plan together, it's often advised to match monthly fixed expenses with defined income sources, like Social Security, pensions, and other annuity income. Beyond these income streams, consider creating an additional bucket of retirement savings to help subsidize any shortfall as well as to provide for lump sum withdrawals for major purchases.

Your Financial Fuel

Many people begin creating a retirement savings strategy when they receive their first full-time job. Employers commonly offer 401(k)s, so starting there makes sense, especially if the company matches your contribution.

Getting time on your side is one of the biggest strategies you can employ as an investor. By starting early, you can invest less money and use compounding interest to help accumulate wealth. Yet, many people aren't disciplined enough to put a plan in place at an early age. Let's walk through a hypothetical example of what could happen.

When Sally is 25 years old, she meets with her advisor because she wants to accumulate $1,000,000 in her investment account by the time she's 65. She wants to know how she can get started. Her advisor tells her that she should invest about $125 per biweekly paycheck into a retirement account and earn a hypothetical 8% return on her investment. Since the money will be contributed pretax, it will feel like less than that to her monthly budget. Sally decides that now is not the right time to start investing and would rather spend her money enjoying her 20s. After all, she's only young once and has the rest of her life to invest.

She comes back to her advisor 10 years later. She's married now and has two kids. She wants to figure out how much she needs to invest now to reach that same $1,000,000 account balance. Her advisor does the calculation and shares with her that she'll need to contribute $335 per biweekly paycheck. That's over 2.5 times what she would have needed to invest just 10 years earlier. She decides that her budget won't support that level of savings and she would rather spend the money on her kids.

Sally comes back at 50 years old and now knows she needs to get serious about her retirement savings. She meets with her advisor, and this time the advisor says that she will need to save about $2,700 per biweekly paycheck to get to that $1,000,000 account balance. Unfortunately for Sally, the amount that she will need to save takes her entire paycheck, so she decides that she will continue to work for the rest of her life. She feels hopeless, bitter, and as though the financial system failed her.

While Sally had many priorities to juggle during her lifetime, a little bit of savings could have gone a long way. If she had only invested some money in her 401(k) at an early age, she could have taken advantage of compound interest and potentially a company match that would have helped her greatly in her retirement years.

Thrift Savings Plan (TSP)

As a federal employee in the FERS program, you not only have access to the pension plan, but also a self-directed retirement program. This is called the Thrift Savings Plan (TSP). The platform allows you to contribute a specific amount to the plan with a matching contribution from the government.

The first 3% is matched dollar for dollar, and the next 2% is matched at $.50 for each dollar. Any amount contributed over 5% will not receive a match. Additionally, you'll receive a 1% automatic government contribution, whether you contribute or not.

Matching contributions must be invested in the traditional TSP account; however, your deferrals may be invested in either the traditional TSP or Roth TSP. You can elect to split your contributions between two accounts, although maximum contribution limits apply to the *combined* contribution amount.

The TSP has five investment options to choose from:

C Fund – Common Stock Index Fund
S Fund – Small Cap Stock Index Fund
I Fund – International Stock Index Fund
F Fund – Fixed Income Index Fund
G Fund – Government Securities Index Fund

There are also five life cycle target date funds (L Funds), which are preset portfolios based on a targeted retirement date. The allocation reduces the amount invested in stock-based funds as the targeted date draws closer.

One concept that the advisor shared with Sally is the Rule of 72. This helps to mathematically calculate how long it will take your investment to double at a specific investment rate. Using the Rule of 72, Sally could estimate how much she'll have in retirement.

If by age 35 Sally had accumulated $100,000 in her retirement account, she could predict that her account would double every 10 years assuming a hypothetical 7.2% rate of return, which would be three times during her remaining working years. Assuming she doesn't contribute any more to the account, her $100,000 compounds to $800,000 by age 65 (assuming that hypothetical 7.2% rate of return). The more years Sally has until she needs her money, the greater the effect of compound interest.

The Rule of 72 is a hypothetical example. It uses a sustained hypothetical rate of return which can act as a shortcut to illustrate how compound interest and rates of return can work for you. There are no guarantees that any investment will sustain the same rate of return year after year, and thus no guarantee that your money will actually double in a stated period of time.

The Rule of 72 has a dark side to it, however. Sally predicts that she will need about $50,000 per year to cover her retirement expenses. What she forgets to factor into her plan is how inflation will affect her budget. The dark side of the Rule of 72 predicts how long it takes for your expenses to double.

Sally estimates that at a 3.36% inflation rate her $50,000 of retirement expenses will double in 21 years. Meaning, Sally will need $100,000 at age 86 to live the same lifestyle as she did when she was 65. Since more and more retirees are living longer due to advances in medicine and healthier lifestyles, accounting for inflation is a major part of a successful retirement plan.

As Sally looks towards some solutions to helping her maintain her retirement lifestyle, she'll want to review all of the products on the market. As she designs her retirement income portfolio, she might want to consider some investment products that were tossed aside during her accumulation years. Instead of growing her portfolio, her objective may have shifted toward preserving the nest egg that she's worked so hard to build. Ultimately, she may plan to take a particular asset and turn it into an income stream.

Annuities play a major part in providing retirees a sense of security. An annuity is a long-term, tax-deferred retirement vehicle that provides guaranteed income you can't outlive. Guarantees are based on the financial strength and claims-paying ability of the issuing company.

When you choose to annuitize, you exchange a lump sum of money for a guaranteed income stream for life. Similar to a pension, generally, there are a variety of payout options. Because you are giving a lump sum of money to an insurance company that underwrites the contract, this strategy possesses drawbacks. You lose the ability to get that money back. At the same time, this vehicle will provide you with the most amount of guaranteed income.

Annuities carry fees and expenses that typically exceed traditionally managed portfolios. They also have deferred sales charges for withdrawals taken too early. For some investors, the guarantees that annuities provide are well worth the cost and restrictions.

Living a Tax-Advantaged Life

Most retirees use 401(k)s and traditional IRAs as their primary investment vehicle for savings. While these accounts provide significant tax benefits on money contributed, they have some major drawbacks. One of the biggest downsides is that withdrawals are 100% taxable as earned income.

As you itemize your retirement income sources, make sure to review the tax liability of each. Between pensions, annuities, withdrawals from pretax retirement accounts, and any income you earn from employment, your taxable income can add up rather quickly. Don't forget to count Social Security too. If your taxable income exceeds a certain threshold, which half of your Social Security check contributes to, then up to 85% of your Social Security benefits can be taxable. Come April 15, the total amount you owe Uncle Sam might surprise you.

Consider using tax-advantaged buckets of money as you build out your retirement plan. Roth IRAs, Roth 401(k)s, and cash value life insurance policies all can be great additions to your investment portfolio. And, withdrawals from these investment vehicles can be taken income tax-free.

Ask yourself if you'd rather live on one completely taxable $100,000 paycheck, or on two paychecks of $50,000 each with one paycheck taxable and one paycheck tax-free. Choosing the second option will lower the amount of tax you owe in retirement. It will also give you greater flexibility since you'll have a pot of money you can access for tax-advantaged lump sum withdrawals.

For example, let's assume that you're retired and looking to buy a new $30,000 car. You want to pay cash but need to figure out where you're going to access the funds. You could withdraw $40,000 from your traditional IRA and send $10,000 straight to the IRS (assuming a 25% withholding), or you could take the $30,000 out of your Roth IRA and not owe taxes on the withdrawal. In the end, by using Roth accounts, you may be able to retire having saved less money since you've removed Uncle Sam as a withdrawal expense.

In addition to using Roth accounts and cash value life insurance to fund your retirement, they can supplement educational expenses. It's generally not recommended to use Roth accounts for a goal other than retirement since the longer you let them sit, the more tax-free growth can accumulate. While the primary purpose to purchase life insurance is for the death benefit, cash value life insurance plans are a universal tool that can be used for a variety of purposes.

Many Americans face the tradeoff of saving for retirement or for college. While you can finance a college education a number of ways, borrowing for your retirement is generally not advised.

Think twice before compromising your retirement savings to fund college. Your intentions are good—you want to help your children with the financial burden of educational expenses. But if your retirement is mismanaged, the burden will come around to your kids anyway when you rely on them to help support you in your later years.

In the end, with proper retirement planning and risk management, the goal is to have a clear path toward achieving lifetime financial security. Your strategy should attempt to build a moat around your financial fortress and to protect your nest-egg from financial uncertainty. Ultimately, your plan can help you attain your vision of retirement and achieve financial freedom.

To be clear, this information should not be considered as tax advice. You should consult your tax advisor regarding your own situation.

Chapter 7
College Planning

Education is the most powerful weapon
which you can use to change the world.
—*Nelson Mandela*

A college education can be the most expensive cost that a young adult will undertake. Whether educational expenses are financed by a parent or other family member, a scholarship, loans, or a student's personal funds, there are many factors to consider when planning for this expense.

College costs are increasing at a rapid rate. Many parents feel that there's no way they can afford this expense on top of all the other demands on their budget. What makes this financial goal even more challenging to plan for is the graduation rate. Not everyone ends up going to college or staying in school once enrolled. A staggering 45% of students who begin college won't finish.[23]

We already know education seriously affects the financial success of the student. Diploma-holding millennials have annual incomes

23 National Student Clearinghouse Research Center – Signature Report - Completing College: A State-Level View of Student Attainment Rates, February 2015, accessed December 09, 2016, https://nscresearchcenter.org/wp-content/uploads/NSC_Signature_Report_8_StateSupp.pdf.

$17,500 greater than those without a college degree. At the same time, planning for this expense is quite challenging. It's difficult to plan when the chance of the goal coming to fruition is about the same as a coin flip. You might think that those numbers don't apply to you and your kids. Your kids might be A students or president of their class. While the statistics include delinquents and bad students, there's more to the story.

There's a variety of reasons why your student may not complete their college curriculum. Some students flounder because they just can't handle the stress or are unclear on a direction. The college atmosphere may not be the right fit and their personality is better suited going straight into the workforce.

On the other hand, your child may find the college atmosphere too fitting. They could be spending too much time on the social aspects of college life, rather than the academics. It's fine to have fun, but a lack of studying could lead to failure.

Many times, students become disinterested in the academics if they're entrepreneurial in nature. They see college as an obstacle to realizing their business aspirations and may decide to leave to pursue those dreams.

Among the ultra-wealthy, college is not always seen as a necessity. In fact, some entrepreneurs and executives believe that college is a waste of time and money. They still see value in the relationships and connections formed during these years but claim that the academic environment stunts growth. Instead, they suggest more practical, hands-on training to help teach skills and develop markets. Whatever your viewpoint, a proper plan should be formulated to address many different outcomes.

Estimating the Cost

As Stephen Covey once said, "Begin with the end in mind." A young couple with a newborn baby will want to begin taking into account the cost of college 18 years in the future. You won't know for sure what college they will attend or if they will go to school at all. Try to make the best guess and model a couple of school options in your planning.

Consider the University of Maryland as an example. The in-state cost for the 2016-17 academic year was $26,525.[24] This includes tuition, room, board, textbooks, and incidental costs. Using an assumed hypothetical 5% inflation rate, one year of college in 2034 will cost $63,836. Over a four-year college career, the total cost adds up to $275,141. It's no wonder that many people give up on saving for college altogether.

Once broken down into a savings strategy, it becomes a bit more reasonable. If you aim to cover 100% of the cost, you'd need to save $530 per month for 21 years and earn an 8% annualized return.

This doesn't account for a variety of factors that could help subsidize the costs. For starters, any gift money that your child receives could be invested in the same account. Factoring in about $500 of gift money per year, drops your contribution to $488 per month.

Furthermore, other loved ones may want to help contribute to this major expense. Many grandparents make special gifts beyond holidays and birthdays toward their grandkids' college. If you're one of the lucky ones on the receiving end, or even on the giving end, be sure to account for this in your plan. For our example, let's not assume any extra gifts toward the savings plan.

You might also forget that when your child goes off to school, you can see some of your monthly budget items go down. Food and utilities should fall with one less individual in the household. Along with this, you may realize that you can afford to pay some of the college costs from cash flow, which we will discuss in more depth later on in the chapter. Going back to our example, let's take $5,000 a year off the top to reflect these budgetary savings. After these reductions, the total monthly investment drops down to $428 per month.

---

[24] "Undergraduate Tuition and Fees, Office of the Bursar, University of Maryland," Undergraduate Tuition and Fees, Office of the Bursar, University of Maryland, accessed December 09, 2016, http://bursar.umd.edu/t_ug1617.php.

This example assumes your child attends the University of Maryland with in-state tuition. Your child might end up going to a private school or an institution out of state. Also, you may start your college savings plan later when your kids are a bit older. Either way, you will need to take the big goal and break it down into bite-size pieces. Try to avoid getting overwhelmed by the size of the bill and make a plan to do what you can.

In our example, we focused on paying 100% of total costs. Many students qualify for financial aid. You might even want your child to have some skin in the game and encourage them to hold a part-time job to pay for incidentals.

College Savings Accounts

After you've created a college savings strategy, you'll need to decide on an account type. Reviewing the potential savings vehicles is an often-overlooked step in executing a strategy. Let's consider a few different ways that you could fund your college savings goals.

Within each of these accounts, you can select investments that fit your risk tolerance. This gives you control of your investment style, allowing you to become more conservative as the date of admission draws closer.

• Custodial Bank Account

As discussed in chapter five, a parent or guardian can create a custodial account on behalf of a minor child. These accounts are sometimes called Uniform Gift to Minors Act (UGMA) or Uniform Transfer to Minors Act (UTMA) accounts. They can be traditional savings accounts held at the bank or can contain investments through a broker.

People choose to save in these accounts for two main reasons: convenience and taxation. It's convenient because banks have low account minimums that make these accounts simple to establish. The account is held in the child's name, so each account is easy to distinguish. From a tax perspective, these accounts are subject to the kiddie tax rules. This provides a certain amount of tax-free income.

While UGMA and UTMA accounts are common, they are not always the best college savings option. While they do provide some benefits, they come with some major limitations as well. If too much money sits in these accounts, the interest earned could be taxed at your income tax rate. Also, when the minor reaches the age of majority, ownership rights transfer, and they can withdraw the funds for any reason they want. Lastly, these accounts are deemed to hold the child's money and thus significantly impact financial aid qualification.

UGMAs and UTMAs are not typically recommended for college savings but are ideal for small savings accounts to teach your child about money and banking.

- **Coverdell Accounts**

Coverdell accounts, also called Educational Savings Accounts (ESAs) or Educational IRAs, are made for educational savings and come with advantageous features. Deposits grow tax-deferred, eliminating the taxation of interest earned each year. Also, if the money is withdrawn for private school or college expenses, it can be accessed tax-free, paying no taxes on any growth. If money is withdrawn for a reason other than paying for qualified education expenses, you may owe taxes and penalties.

ESA balances are held in the parent's name for the benefit of the child. This provides additional safeguards for parents on how the funds may be accessed. Since the funds rest in an account intended for educational expenses, they are considered in the financial aid calculation but not as heavily as custodial accounts.

One more advantage of the ESA is that funds may be available for private schooling prior to college. Keep in mind that there are maximum contribution limits, as well as restrictions based on the income level of the donor so it may be hard to accumulate significant balances for college in this vehicle.

- **529 Plans**

A 529 plan is a tax-advantaged investment program designed to help pay for qualified higher education costs. Being one of the most popular ways to save for college, the 529 plan comes in two flavors: prepaid tuition plans (only offered in select states) and savings plans.

With prepaid plans, you can purchase tuition at today's rates instead of the inflated rates when your child is ready to go to school. There are some dangers in doing this. For one, if your child doesn't enroll in a school within the state where you established the plan, you may not be able to transfer the credits for full value. If your child doesn't go to college, it might be impossible to transfer your credits to another child, depending on your resident state. These plans generally allow you to prepay tuition only, so eventually you would also pay additional costs associated with attending college.

With the 529 savings plan, the investment risk, including the potential for loss of principal, and the contribution commitments shift to you. Participation in a 529 plan does not guarantee that the contributions and investment returns will be adequate to cover higher education expenses. But if you need flexibility in contributions or think investing your money may provide a higher rate of return to beat out tuition inflation, this type of account may work for you.

These savings plans are similar to ESAs, but to qualify for tax-free withdrawals, the money must be used for post-secondary educational expenses. If you make withdrawals for nonqualified expenses, you'll need to pay taxes and penalties on any investment gains. These accounts are transferable to other related children, so if your child receives a scholarship or decides not to attend school altogether, you can transfer the funds to another beneficiary.

One other important difference with the ESA is that the maximum contribution is much lower than for the 529 plan. Since contributions to a 529 plan are considered gifts, the maximum contribution is tied to the annual gift exclusion limit. At the same time, you can "hyper-contribute," or use five years of contributions to start the plan. This will allow you to jump-start the plan with a large lump sum but disqualify you from making annual contributions over the following five years.

529 plans are generally state-sponsored. Your state of residence may offer state tax advantages to residents who participate in the plan, all of course are subject to meeting certain conditions or requirements. If you decide to contribute to a different state's 529 plan, then you may miss out on certain state tax advantages. The state that you choose to set your 529 plan up with doesn't have any bearing on the ability to access funds tax-free. For example, you could set up a Maryland 529 plan but use the funds to pay for the University of North Carolina. There are even some educational institutions overseas that qualify as well, although the list is limited.

Any state-based benefits should be one of many appropriately weighted factors to consider when making an investment decision. You should consult with your financial advisor or tax advisor to learn more about how state-based benefits (including any limitations) would apply to your specific circumstances. You may also wish to contact your state's 529 plan program administrator to learn more about the benefits that might be available to you by investing in the in-state plan.

If you're married, consider opening two accounts for each child to take full advantage of these state tax deductions: Both parents can open separate accounts for each child. Depending on your state, this could allow you to double the amount of the state tax deduction available.

While the 529 plan is a good account to fund college costs, they do have some drawbacks. Overfunding your educational savings goal with this investment vehicle might prove problematic since funds must be used for qualified educational expenses to receive the tax benefits. For financial aid purposes, 529 plans can impact the calculation. If you have only one child, or if you believe your kids will be receiving scholarships, then these vehicles might not be the right fit.

- ## Life Insurance

Another option is to use cash value life insurance for supplemental college funding. Since life insurance cash values can be accessed during your lifetime for any reason without taxes or penalties, there is no need to prove you are using the money for college.

If your child ends up receiving scholarship funds or doesn't attend school, you can withdraw the money for something else or keep the funds to supplement your own retirement. Cash value life insurance is not required to be reported in the financial aid calculation. This can be a huge advantage and may help you to maximize your financial aid package.

Using cash value life insurance may not be for everyone. If you don't otherwise need or want life insurance, you'll encounter unnecessary insurance expenses and possible restrictions, such as surrender charges, that can impede growth. At the same time, if life insurance is needed, costs can be minimized by combining the two objectives into one vehicle.

Keep in mind that the primary reason for purchasing life insurance is the death benefit. However, the growth of cash value is tax-deferred, and the money can be withdrawn in a way that limits your tax liability. Any outstanding loans or withdrawals may create additional taxes in the event of a lapse or policy surrender and will reduce both cash value and death benefit, so make sure to consult with your advisor on how to design the right type of policy for your situation.

- ## Alternative Vehicles

You can find many other investment vehicles that traditionally aren't used to save for college, yet these funds may work for you if needed. Roth IRAs have risen in popularity over the years because of the tax-free withdrawal benefits for retirees. If used to pay for qualified education expenses for certain individuals, you may avoid the 10% early withdrawal penalty. You may incur income tax liability on at least part of the amount distributed, still.

Using a Roth IRA as a college savings vehicle is usually not advised since you are susceptible to taxes. Also, since you're tapping the funds early, there is an opportunity cost based on what the funds' growth could have been if they had been left alone.

Another strategy is to take a loan against your 401(k) plan for college. Some retirement plans will allow you to take loans and pay them back over a number of years. Any loan interest assessed usually goes right back into your account. Since it's a loan, there are no taxes on the money removed. Repayment of the loan must occur within five years, and loan repayments are not considered plan contributions. Loans are not taxable unless they fail to meet repayment terms, in which case they are treated as a distribution and are taxed as such.

Along with that, if you leave your job with a loan still outstanding, you may owe taxes and penalties on the balance. You must pay back all the funds within sixty days of termination to avoid these penalties. Needleless to say, taking a loan from your retirement plan is not an ideal strategy to pay for college because you are missing out on the potential time value of money.

Some people see real estate as a potential college savings strategy as well. Parents might look to purchase an investment property as a way of leveraging the money they have into an income-producing asset. Instead of investing $50,000 in the stock market, the money could serve as a down payment on an investment property to purchase a $250,000 home. Over the years, you could receive rental income, and when the child leaves for school, the property could be sold, ideally for a higher value. While there are some potential tax benefits to this strategy, there are some major drawbacks.

One of the biggest challenges is that the investment property is not a liquid asset. Depending on the housing market when you need the funds, the house could sit on the market waiting for a buyer. Another challenge is that you will have signed up to become a landlord, bringing with it the headaches of dealing with tenants and unforeseen maintenance expenses. This can put undue pressure on your budget as well as your time.

In the end, keeping your college savings strategy simple and straightforward will give you confidence that you are progressing toward your goal while being mindful of the tax benefits.

Consult your financial advisor for more information on how to customize a college savings strategy that fits your budget and circumstances without compromising your other financial goals. Finally, please remember to check with your individual tax advisor on the tax benefits or impact to your specific situation.

Keep in mind that this is one part of your family's financial plan. Many parents tend to put their children first and save for college before, or instead of, their own retirement savings. This is a big financial no-no. You can always take out loans for college, but you can't take out loans for retirement—nor would you want to.

Chapter 8
Life Insurance

It is not death that a man should fear,
but he should fear never beginning to live.
—Marcus Aurelius

Many of us don't want to think about our deaths and contemplate what would happen if we were no longer around. It's so important to make plans in advance to care for our families. The grief they experience will be more than enough without the added financial struggles. Luckily, there is a solution.

At its core, life insurance is a contract that you form with an insurance company, where, as long as you pay your premiums, the company promises to pay your beneficiaries a sum of money upon your death. But it's so much more than that.

Life insurance death benefits could provide a college education for your kids. It could mean job security for your employees, a lifestyle for your loved ones, and a legacy for your heirs. In short, life insurance is peace of mind.

Life insurance acts as a safety net, ensuring that your financial plan can continue if you or your spouse are no longer around. According to the Life Insurance and Market Research Association (LIMRA), over 40% of Americans do not own a life insurance policy. Most Americans who decide against purchasing life insurance blame cost. Interestingly enough, the same study found that 80% of consumers misjudge the price for term life insurance, with Millennials overestimating the cost by 213% and Gen Xers overestimating the cost by 119%. [25]

Misconceptions abound in the world of insurance and not only related to price. Most Americans are underinsured. The same LIMRA study found that 30% of Americans believed they needed more insurance and 43% stated that they would feel a financial impact within six months if a primary wage earner passed away.

Along with these misconceptions, there are so many different types of life insurance that sorting through them could scare someone into inaction. Add to that the skepticism that the public has for insurance companies and it's not hard to see why we face these challenges.

How Much Is Enough?

One of the first places to start designing your life insurance strategy is to figure out how much is enough. It certainly will depend on a variety of factors. If you are using the coverage to protect your family, there are two ways to calculate the amount needed, using a Human Life Value calculation or a Needs Analysis approach.

The government created the Human Life Value calculation for the families of the victims of the 9/11 attacks. The formula takes the present value of all future income earning years and subtracts that from the present value of the amount of annual household expenses attributable to that person.

---

[25] *2015 Insurance Barometer Study*, LIMRA, accessed December 09, 2016, http://www.orgcorp.com/wp-content/uploads/2015-Insurance-Barometer.pdf.

For example, a 40-year-old earning $100,000 per year and spending $30,000 per year on food, clothes, and household expenses, would have a Human Life Value of about $2 million. Remember, this calculator takes all future income and subtracts all future expenses. This calculation looks only at the individual's value to the household and doesn't address the family's financial position.

The second way to calculate how much life insurance a family might need is through a Needs Analysis approach. Don't let the name fool you; this calculation should be based on your wants, not only your needs. If you were to pass away, you probably wouldn't want your family just scraping by. With this formula, we take a more granular look at the household's financial position. It factors in items such as paying off the mortgage and other debts, child care costs, college funding, retirement savings, final expenses, and emergency reserves.

Let's take the same 40-year-old from the example above. This household situation might call for $1.35 million of life insurance to cover the following items: paying off a $400,000 mortgage, child care costs of $20,000 per year for ten years, $200,000 to send two kids to college, $500,000 to fund a retirement account for the spouse, and $50,000 for end-of-life expenses and emergency reserves. Because each of these items differ from household to household, this calculator can custom fit for each family's specific situation.

We often get caught up in the numbers and lose perspective. If you can't figure out exactly how much you want to cover for certain items, that's okay. It's better to overestimate the amount than underestimate.

Also, try not to dwell on the cost. Once you're approved for coverage, you can go back and amend it for a different amount that will fit your current budget. Finally, if your family has a stay-at-home parent, purchasing a policy on his or her life is critical to the sustainability of the household's success. If that person were no longer around, either the surviving spouse or hired help would need to cover those duties.

What about coverage for nontraditional families? Maybe you're divorced, widowed, or a legal guardian for someone else's children. Life insurance is critical in ensuring that your wishes will be carried out and that your kids will have a strong financial support system.

For example, if you are a single parent and have identified your brother as a potential guardian for your kids if you were no longer around, you'll want to double-check that your brother has the financial capacity to care for your children. Life insurance can provide that support. Whoever you choose as the beneficiary of your policy, you'll want to coordinate with your estate plan. It's important to note that the beneficiary designations of your policy will supersede instructions expressed in your will.

Life insurance products contain fees, such as mortality and expense charges, and may contain restrictions, such as surrender periods. All guarantees are based on the financial strength and claims-paying ability of the issuing insurance company, so selecting a reputable insurance company is important.

Types of Life Insurance

Now that we've identified how much life insurance is enough, we need to select the right type of policy to match our goals. This process can get quite confusing, so make sure to also work with a professional to choose the right fit for your situation.

- **Group Life**

Life insurance can be either employer provided or individually owned. Many employers provide a small amount of life insurance as part of their benefits package. Because companies can deduct the premiums on the first $50,000 of coverage, this is the most common amount offered.

Some employers will give you the option to buy more coverage through the group plan with little or no medical underwriting. This means you won't need to take a physical proving that you're in good health. Depending on the plan and your health, you'll want to evaluate the costs alongside buying the coverage individually.

Many insurance companies offer buy-up rates based on average health and smoker status. If you're healthy and a nonsmoker, it may be more cost-effective to take a physical exam and buy your own policy. Oftentimes, group insurance is not portable when you leave your job or retire.

Federal Employee Group Life Insurance (FEGLI)[26]

As a federal employee, you are eligible for FEGLI coverage. The program provides you with multiples of your income with a variety of different buy-up levels. Premiums are set based upon the age of the insured and increase every five years. Rates are based on average health and smoking status. Consider pricing out an individually underwritten policy, as rates might be significantly less expensive if you are healthy and a nonsmoker.

Basic – This coverage provides 1X your salary rounded up to the next even $1,000 plus an additional $2,000. If you're under the age of 45, you may qualify for an extra benefit, giving you up to twice your salary. The extra benefit is reduced by 10% per year between the ages of 35 and 45.

Option A – The standard plan provides a flat $10,000 of additional coverage beyond the basic plan.

Option B – The additional plan allows you to buy-up to five times your salary, rounding up to the next even $1,000.

Option C – The family plan provides up to $25,000 of coverage for a spouse and up to $12,500 of coverage for any unmarried, dependent child under the age of 22.

---

[26] Federal Employees' Group Life Insurance (FEGLI) Program Handbook, April 2014, accessed December 09, 2016, https://www.opm.gov/healthcare-insurance/life-insurance/reference-materials/handbook.pdf.

• Term Vs. Permanent Life

If you do decide to buy your own policy, you'll likely consider whether to purchase term coverage or a form of permanent life insurance. Purchasing a term policy is similar to renting an apartment. The cost is usually low, it's for a temporary period, and you aren't building any equity in it.

A permanent life policy is like owning a home. The premiums you pay might be a bit higher than for a term policy, but you have coverage for a longer period of time, and you're building equity inside the policy that you can access during your lifetime.

Which kind of policy to buy is not necessarily an either-or conversation. Many times it makes sense to purchase both together to satisfy different purposes.

For example, let's say you figure out that you want a total of $1 million of life insurance coverage. You know you don't want to fund the entire amount through permanent life since you won't need that much after your kids are grown. At the same time, you would like to keep some coverage in your later years. Because you've done your homework, you realize that permanent life can have some major tax benefits, and you would like to use the cash value as a supplemental retirement savings tool. With all of this in mind, you could decide to purchase a $750,000 20-year term plan and a $250,000 permanent plan.

• Whole Life

What kind of permanent plan should you purchase? If you'd prefer a guaranteed death benefit and cash accumulation as a secondary feature, then whole life insurance might be a good fit. Whole life insurance is the strongest of the different types of permanent life because it is basically a contractual guarantee. Under the policy, the company promises to pay the death benefit as long as you continue to pay your fixed premium. The contract can be somewhat inflexible as premiums are fixed for life. The insurance company needs your premiums to provide the guarantee. These policies build cash value and can potentially pay a dividend based on the mortality estimates of the company.

- **Universal Life**

If whole life insurance doesn't fit your style, don't abandon permanent life plans just yet. Universal life insurance was created as whole life's more flexible cousin, allowing the policy owner to control the premium payments and therefore the amount of cash value. You may pay the minimum, maximum, or somewhere in between. Why would anyone want to pay more than the minimum, you ask? Well, any premium over the minimum amount gets allocated in the cash value of the policy and could potentially grow with some tax benefits.

Universal life insurance isn't only for those individuals focused on accumulating assets. The policy can act like whole life and be used primarily for its death benefit. Since universal life is a lot more flexible than whole life, the base policy doesn't usually come with death benefit guarantees. As a result, the life insurance company has the right to come back and ask you for more money later to retain your policy benefits, if they experience adverse mortality expectations.

Many times insurance companies will offer a secondary guarantee as a rider to the policy at an additional cost and potentially with additional restrictions. This rider protects you from the insurance company raising your policy rates. These technical aspects are the main reason it's so critical to do your homework on the insurance company before you buy your policy.

There are three flavors of universal life insurance, and each differs in how the cash values are allocated. These three types are fixed, variable, and indexed. If you end up feeling lost because of all the different types of coverage and additional riders, remember you are purchasing the policy primarily for its death benefit. Stay focused on this, and as you review the different bells and whistles, scrutinize them through this filter. At the end of the day, remember that you're buying discounted dollars for future delivery.

Life Insurance Companies

Now that you know how much coverage to purchase and what type of policy you will use to meet your goal, you'll need to decide on a company to underwrite the insurance. This decision should not be taken lightly because you need the insurer to be around when you are not.

Consumers often look strictly at the price when they compare term quotes. While term life is sometimes viewed as a commodity, evaluating the pros and the cons of each company in relation to your specific situation will give you the best outcome.

Rating agencies—such as A.M. Best, Standard and Poor's, Moody's Investor Service, and Fitch Ratings—independently review the financial strength and stability of an insurance company. They each have different metrics and rating systems, and sometimes they even disagree about a company's outlook.

As a result, you might want to review companies by their Comdex score. The Comdex score is an average percentile that measures company rankings, making it easier to compare companies. Comdex looks at companies ranked by independent rating agencies, ranks more than 200 of those companies on a scale from one (lowest) to one hundred (highest), based on their agency ratings. A company must be rated by at least two rating agencies to receive a Comdex ranking.

It's also a good idea to know whether a company is a stock or mutually owned insurance company. A stock-based company is owned by shareholders and, as a result, makes business decisions that aim to please those individuals. Since their goal is to maximize quarterly profits, they might have more incentives to take risks.

Mutually owned insurance companies are owned by the policyholders, and those companies tend to make business decisions that aim to please them. They might also give policyholders more privileges, like providing voting rights on management personnel and policy decisions.

As you narrow the field to your final choice on an insurance company, consider a couple other items. You'll want a company with a strong history of paying claims. Knowing that a company has been around for decades, or even longer, might be a good sign that they've successfully navigated through some tough economic climates.

Also, you might decide to purchase a term policy now, knowing that one day you'll want to convert to a permanent product. You'll want to select a company with a diverse array of innovative products. This will give you a variety of choices when it comes time to convert.

A Versatile Tool

Many people view life insurance as simply a product to protect their family in the event they pass away too soon. It does provide this peace of mind, yet it can be so much more. Consider the following ways we can incorporate life insurance in a financial plan.

- **Cash Value Accumulation**

While the primary purpose of life insurance is to provide a death benefit, some policies also offer cash value accumulation. Premiums paid toward these policies can vary based on the desires of the policy owner.

You may decide to pay the minimum amount and focus solely on a guaranteed death benefit. Other times, you may want to use the policy as a cash accumulation tool. By contributing to the policy beyond the mortality and expense charges, your premiums increase the cash value of the policy. This investment can have substantial tax benefits and can be accessed during your lifetime through loans and withdrawals. Keep in mind that policy loans and withdrawals may create an adverse tax result, in the event of a lapse or policy surrender, and will reduce both the cash value and death benefit.

Some people use this strategy to supplement paying for long-term goals, such as college or even retirement. Be careful not to contribute too much to these accounts because the IRS may then classify your policy as a Modified Endowment Contract (or MEC), and you may jeopardize the tax benefits. If a policy is over funded and becomes a MEC, the contract's earnings will be taxed as ordinary income at withdrawal and may be subject to a 10% penalty if withdrawn before age 59 ½. You can avoid a policy becoming a MEC if it's designed correctly. Be sure to work with a financial professional to construct a policy for your specific goals.

- **Key Employee Insurance**

If you're a business owner and have a few employees critical to the success and sustainability of the company, you might want to protect yourself in case something happens to them. Life insurance can be a great tool, as it will provide the company financial support to replace the key employee in the event of an untimely passing.

Some business owners use permanent life insurance to fulfill this need since they can also use it as a "golden handcuff" or incentive to encourage the employee to stay with the company. You can have a professional draft an agreement that obligates the business owner to pay a lump sum if the key employee stays for a certain number of years. That amount can be funded using a permanent life insurance contract.

If the key employee dies or leaves before they have fulfilled their end of the agreement, the business owner has either the death benefit or the cash value of the policy to help in replacing that individual. If the key employee does fulfill their obligation, the employee can either liquidate the policy or simply take over as owner and use it as their own asset. This agreement between the business owner and key employee helps the business owner retain the employee and protect themselves if that employee were to die or leave.

- **Leaving a Legacy**

Some individuals who own large assets, like a small business, land, or even a family house, might want to pass these items to the next generation as a legacy. Without proper estate planning, these items might need to be liquidated by the heirs to pay estate taxes. If the value of your total estate exceeds a certain threshold, it may be subject to estate taxes on the amount over that threshold. Those taxes must be paid in cash, which could result in the need to sell your legacy. Life insurance can be a great resource to provide cash at such times.

This is what happened with the Washington Redskins in the 1990s. The team was sold at a steep discount to Daniel Snyder, to come up with the cash to pay the estate taxes. Had the former owner, Jack Kent Cooke, purchased life insurance, his children would have inherited the team and could have kept it or sold it later for a much higher value.

While you may not own a sports franchise, you might have a business or plot of land that you want to remain intact and within the family upon your passing. Life insurance can help ensure that you achieve the legacy as you wish.

- **Charitable Aspirations**

If you are charitably inclined or have a specific organization or cause you would like to help fund, life insurance can help. Some people want to be sure that even if they've used up all their money during their lifetime, when they die, some amount can be donated to a specific cause. Naming charitable organizations as the beneficiaries of a life insurance policy will give them funds to help their long-term missions while allowing you to make a significant impact even after you pass.

A little bit can go a long way. Some people don't give to charity because they think their small donation won't make much of a difference. Instead of giving the donation directly to the charity, consider using your contribution to purchase a life insurance policy. Now, your dollars are going toward a larger amount, giving you confidence that you can make a significant impact after you pass.

Whether it's a local church or a state university, most organizations have a person or entire department to help with the donations process. Make sure you work with these people to coordinate your plan with theirs. They need to know your plan as they make preparations for funding their long-term projects. You also might qualify for certain perks while you're living, as a thank you for your future donations.

As you review life insurance's role in your overall plan, don't forget what you're truly doing. You're giving your kids a college education, your employees job security, and your family a lifestyle. Ultimately, you're creating financial freedom.

Chapter 9
Disability & Long Term Care Insurance

Health is not valued till sickness comes.
—*Thomas Fuller*

What is your greatest asset? Is it your house? Your retirement account? Maybe a business? For many, your greatest asset is your income earning potential. Think about it. A 40-year-old with an annual income of $100,000 could earn more than $2.5 million over the rest of their working career. That doesn't even factor in any raises or bonuses.

What would happen if you could no longer bring in that paycheck? The majority of Americans are just scraping by each month and living paycheck to paycheck. It's no wonder that medical problems contributed to 62% of all personal bankruptcies in 2007[27] and half of all home foreclosures in 2006.[28]

---

[27] David U. Himmelstein, M.D. et al., "Medical Bankruptcy in the United States, 2007: Results of a National Study," The American Journal of Medicine 122, no. 8 (August 2009).

[28] Christopher Tarver Robertson, Richard Egelhof, and Michael Hoke, "Get Sick, Get Out: The Medical Causes for Home Mortgage," accessed December 09, 2016, http://scholarlycommons.law.case.edu/cgi/viewcontent.cgi?article=1210&context=healthmatrix.

If the ability to earn an income is such a critical piece of people's financial plans, why don't they insure it? The Council for Disability Awareness found that employees believe their odds of becoming disabled for at least three months was a mere 1%.[29] In reality, its probability is more like 25% for today's 20-year-olds[30].

Do you think Social Security will cover you in case of disability? In 2012, 65% of initial Social Security Disability Insurance claim applications were denied.[31] This is simply not a viable option and puts even more pressure on the consumers to understand the risks. It can get quite complicated to wade through group benefits and supplemental policies.

To make matters worse, people frequently confuse disability and long term care insurance. Both programs trigger claims in the event of adverse health conditions. Where they differ is that disability insurance protects an income stream and long term care insurance covers the cost of a caregiver.

Types of Disability

There are many different types of disability that could impair your ability to work. Many people think that becoming a quadriplegic is what it would take to become disabled, but that's not necessarily the case.

A disability may not mean a physical impairment. A bout of depression or anxiety, could make performing job duties challenging. It doesn't have to be a permanent impairment either. Maybe you were in a bad car collision and need to take nine months off for physical therapy. Or, what if you could still go to work, just not for the full 40 hours per week.

---

[29] The Disability Divide: Employer Study (Council for Disability Awareness, 2013), 6, accessed December 09, 2016, http://disabilitycanhappen.org/research/pdfs/employerresearch2013.pdf.

[30] US Social Security Administration, Fact Sheet February 7, 2013.

[31] US Social Security Administration, Disabled Worker Beneficiary Data Statistics by Calendar Year, December 2012, accessed December 09, 2016, https://www.ssa.gov/oact/STATS/dibStat.html.

The Council for Disability Awareness found that the top five causes of new disability insurance claims[32] were:

1. Muscle/Bone Disorders
2. Cancer
3. Accidents
4. Mental Disorders
5. Cardiovascular

While the items on the list seem broad, they relate to a variety of conditions that could impact your financial plan in a big way. For example, remember that old sports injury from high school? It's not a big deal now, but it could come back or cause another condition later.

What about the baby blues? According to the Centers for Disease Control and Prevention, 11–20% of women who give birth each year have postpartum depression symptoms.[33] These symptoms could be so severe that they impact the ability for the new mother to return to work.

Employer-Provided Benefits

Many employers provide disability insurance as part of their employee benefits packages. While these programs can be a great start, they should not be relied upon to fulfill the entire need should a disability arise. A typical long-term disability plan might cover 60% of your income up to a $5,000 per month cap. While this sounds like a nice benefit, consider how your lifestyle would be affected if your boss asked you to take a 40% pay cut. Add to that any out-of-pocket medical bills related to your disability, and you can start to see how this benefit may not be enough.

The cap placed on these benefits can impact you in a big way. With this example, a $5,000 per month cap equals $60,000 per year of

---

[32] 2013 Long Term Disability Claims Review, 6, accessed December 09, 2016, http://www.disabilitycanhappen.org/research/CDA_LTD_Claims_Survey_2013.pdf.

[33] "Depression Among Women," Centers for Disease Control and Prevention, 2016. accessed December 10, 2016, https://www.cdc.gov/reproductivehealth/depression/.

maximum benefits. As your salary increases beyond $100,000 per year, the total percentage of your income covered actually declines.

Consider a manager who makes $125,000 per year. In the event of a disability, the payout could be capped at $5,000 per month or 48% of their gross income. To make matters worse, group disability benefits are usually taxed, lowering the effective coverage percentage to about 35% of gross income. That's a significant drop in pay.

Federal Employee Disability Retirement

For those who work for the federal government, disability benefits are provided by the Federal Employee Retirement System (FERS) and must be studied carefully. If you have an illness or injury that takes you out of work, you'll need to apply for Disability Retirement. You don't actually become eligible for these benefits until after you've served 18 months.

Once you make a claim, you'll have to wait 180 days before you begin to receive benefits, so be sure to have enough money earmarked in your emergency reserves to last this long without a paycheck. You'll receive 60% of your income the first year you're disabled. The payout then drops to 40% for every year beyond that. Disability retirement will pay only until age 62, at which time you will begin receiving your federal pension.

To go on claim, or receive benefits, you must be completely disabled. If you can work part-time, you will no longer be eligible for these benefits. Furthermore, the FERS Disability income is offset by any other social income source, whether from Social Security Disability or a private policy that you own with a Social Security offset rider.

Consider supplementing FERS Disability program with an individually underwritten policy. If you're healthy, you can apply through a private insurance company to layer in additional coverage that could potentially pay out, even if you can go back to work part time.

Purchasing Your Own Policy

After reviewing your disability benefits at work, you may decide to supplement with a private insurance policy. As you review what's available beyond what your employer offers, it's important to understand all the provisions and purchase the policy that works best for you and your circumstances.

One of the most important provisions is the definition of disability. This is the metric by which the insurance company will consider you disabled and pay out a claim. There are two major classifications of a disability: Any occupation and own occupation.

If your policy uses an "any occupation" provision, the policy benefits will payout only if you have been disabled so severely that you can no longer work in *any* occupation. An alternative definition of disability would be "own occupation." This provision states that the policy will pay out a claim if you are disabled and can no longer work in your *own* occupation. You may still be able to perform the duties of another job, so this policy allows you to go on claim, or collect benefits, while still being able to work but not in your usual capacity.

An example of when you might want to have the own occupation definition of disability is if you're an attorney and begin to experience symptoms of anxiety. Although you may no longer be able to work in your own occupation because of the high-pressure environment, you could work as a teacher. Having a policy with an own occupation definition of disability could allow you to go on claim and receive benefits while still being able to work in some capacity.

You may decide to purchase a policy with residual benefits. This allows you to receive benefits even if you return to work part time. Many insurance companies will pay a fraction of the benefits based on the amount of time you are out. If you can work for only 20 hours per week, for example, then you may be eligible for half of the benefits.

Another common provision to consider is an inflation rider. This add-on will increase your benefits by a specific cost-of-living metric each year once you are on claim. If you're early in your career, consider adding this feature to protect your lifetime earnings potential. It's important that benefit dollars continue to maintain the same purchasing power to pay your bills.

As you decide how much coverage to purchase, keep in mind that benefits are typically received tax-free since you are unable to deduct the premiums you pay for the insurance. At the same time, if you are self-employed, you do have the option to deduct the premiums. If you decide to do this, just know that any benefits that you receive will be taxable.

Long Term Care

Unlike disability insurance, individuals need long term care when they can no longer care for themselves. Usually, this is when you can no longer perform at least two of the six "activities of daily living." These include bathing, continence, dressing, eating, toileting, or transferring (for example moving from your bed to a chair). A mental incapacity, such as Alzheimer's disease, might also trigger long term care.

A variety of settings and people can offer needed care. The most common place is nursing home care, which provides skilled care, rehabilitation services, and help with daily living activities. Nowadays, more and more people are opting for in-home care to maintain a level of comfort and familiarity. Caregivers can be hired to provide these services at home and may be supplemented with help from family or friends.

Adult daycare centers provide activities during the day, often with pickup and drop off services. This can be advantageous for those who live at home either by themselves or with family members who work during the day. The daycare centers promote a variety of health, social, and related support services during the day.

Finally, there's hospice care. This can be in-home or in a facility. Hospice care centers help chronically or terminally ill patients ease their symptoms. Care may also focus on providing emotional and spiritual support.

Paying the Price

There are a variety of ways to cover the costs associated with long term care services. Some people believe that Medicare will cover these expenses. Although Medicare will cover the costs of skilled care in a hospital, it does so in a limited capacity. The first 20 days are fully covered, and the next 80 days are covered after a daily deductible is paid. Medicare will not cover further long term care costs beyond those one hundred days.

Medicaid is another program that people look to for coverage of long-term care costs. Medicaid is primarily for the impoverished people of our country. To qualify for the program, many states require you to spend down your assets and income sources to a very low threshold. Some people consider giving money and other assets to family members to qualify; however, beware of the five-year look-back period, which penalizes you for any assets over a certain threshold gifted within five years of applying for Medicaid.

If you do qualify for Medicaid, you will be eligible for government-sponsored long term care programs. Every state regulates their programs, so there may be limitations on services provided and living conditions may not be desirable. As a result, turning to Medicaid as your primary long term care strategy might not provide you with choices that align with your desires.

Whether on purpose or not, without a proper plan, these expenses fall on you or your family. This may be a viable option if you have substantial savings and you're comfortable with absorbing the cost of care. However, for many retirees, these expenses will wipe out their entire life savings, leaving little left for a spouse or children.

You may choose to seek private insurance as a strategy to help cover long term care expenses. Purchasing a long term care insurance policy can shift some or all this burden off your shoulders. With rising rates, high costs, and complicated jargon, these plans can be difficult to evaluate. Don't throw the baby out with the bathwater, though.

The long term care insurance marketplace continues to evolve with new products coming into the market all the time. These new products address many of retirees' biggest concerns. They also provide options that fit nicely into a comprehensive financial plan. Ultimately, a long term care policy can protect your nest egg in the event you need care.

As with all other types of insurance, it's important to align yourself with an agent you trust and who knows your specific set of circumstances. Expert advice to shop the marketplace for the right product designed to fit your situation will bring you peace of mind.

Both disability and long term care insurance are commonly overlooked by consumers. Review how a catastrophic event could impact your overall financial plan. Adding this coverage to your insurance arsenal could save you a substantial amount of money and hours of worry.

Chapter 10
Health Insurance

It is health that is real wealth and not pieces of gold and silver.
—Mahatma Gandhi

Health insurance is one of the most politically controversial financial products on the market. Many people don't understand how it works and don't know how to choose the right type of coverage.

Health insurance is generally an employer-provided benefit. It's common for your human resources (HR) director to provide a few different options in packages from which you can choose. Your company may subsidize part of the premiums so that the premiums you pay are a fraction of the whole.

Selecting from the limited options available can be challenging. Although more choices can increase complexity, narrowing the choices to three options seems logical. At the same time, you lose flexibility and customization. Not everyone fits into plan A, B, or C. Be careful as you choose a plan that it fits your unique situation as closely as possible.

The Nuts and Bolts

When you purchase major medical health insurance, you enter into a contract with a company. They will work on your behalf to pay for covered health products and services. These items can range from a routine doctor's visit all the way to major surgery. Doctors submit their bills to your insurance company, which then decides how much of the charges are reasonable.

For example, let's assume you go to the doctor for a consult, and they submit a bill of $200 to your insurance for the visit. The insurance company reviews the bill and decides that $120 of the $200 is reasonable for the services rendered. At this point, the $120 is applied to your insurance plan. You will pay all, none, or a portion of the bill, depending on your coverage.

Many doctor visits are covered with copays. These are rates your insurance company has set that dictate your share of the cost of covered services. In the example above, the insurance company considered $120 a reasonable cost for the visit. If your insurance policy imposes a $30 copay, you would pay $30, and the insurance company would cover the remaining $90 of the reasonable cost.

Deductible is the next term you might hear as you compare health insurance plans. A deductible is a set amount of eligible costs that you are responsible to pay before the insurance begins paying for your health care. Covered services that are subject to deductibles do not usually incur copays. These services may include hospital stays, surgical procedures, x-rays, and even prescription drugs. Your deductible might range anywhere from $0 all the way up to $10,000. Keep in mind that the lower the deductible, the higher your monthly premium.

Throughout the calendar year, as you pay for health care services, you may spend enough to exceed your deductible. At this point, a coinsurance factor kicks in. This is the formula (expressed as percentages) that the insurance company uses to split the covered expenses with you. Often, this rate favors you. For example, if you've had some major health care expenses that total $10,000. You'll pay

100% of expenses up to your $2,000 deductible. The remaining $8,000 is split between you and the insurance company 80/20. After the deductible, you'd be responsible for covering an additional $1,600, and the insurance company would pay the other $6,400.

At some point, you may incur a large amount of health care expenses that exceed your out-of-pocket maximum. This is the absolute most you are responsible for paying for your health care expenses in any given year.

For example, we'll assume the out-of-pocket maximum on your plan is $5,000. Let's say you incurred $20,000 of bills for the birth of your child. Using the same example as before, you'd pay 100% of the $2,000 deductible and 20% coinsurance for remaining expenses ($15,000 x .20 = $3,000) up to an out-of-pocket maximum of $5,000. All future expenses incurred during that calendar year will be covered 100% by the insurance company since you are over the out-pocket maximum.

There can be different deductible and out-of-pocket maximum limits for individuals as well as families. Be sure to understand the inner workings of your plan and your family's unique needs before selecting one that fits your situation.

Dental and vision coverage are usually itemized separately from other covered services. Sometimes a different insurance carrier will underwrite these types of plans. As a result, they usually have their own provisions for coverage and don't coordinate with major medical coverage.

When you are trying to choose the right policy, all of these different features and options can be confusing. As you make your decision, try to evaluate your family's situation. Are you actively seeking medical attention for a chronic condition? Are you on any long-term medications? Do you foresee a major health event coming soon? Do you go to see doctors only if it's an emergency?

You may want to also make a list of your health care expenses from the prior year to get an idea of your spending on healthcare.

Compare this list with what you might need going into the next year to help choose the right health plan for you.

Leaving Your Job?

Nearly 56% of non-elderly Americans receive health benefits from their employer.[34] If you suffer a job loss or decide to make a change willingly, you might find yourself stuck with few options to keep your coverage.

Under the Consolidated Omnibus Budget Reconciliation Act of 1985 (COBRA), an employee is entitled to continue their health coverage after leaving employment. Usually, this is limited to 18 months past your termination date. Since premiums will no longer be subsidized by your company, your premiums will probably rise.

If retaining your health insurance plan through your former employer costs too much for your budget, you have the option of purchasing your own policy. You can purchase a plan through your state's insurance exchange or a private health insurance agent. Plans range from full major medical coverage to transitional health care policies that bridge the gap between employers.

Tax-Advantaged Plans

Trends in health insurance parallel what happened with retirement plans over the last 30–40 years. With retirement plans, more of the burden has been placed on consumers to self-direct and manage their own retirement funds through 401(k)s, with a decreased emphasis on guaranteed pensions. Similarly, insurance companies now emphasize the self-management of health care funds through high-deductible plans, health savings accounts (HSAs), and flexible spending account (FSAs).

---

[34] 2016 Sep 14, "2016 Employer Health Benefits Survey," Kaiser Family Foundation - Health Policy Research, Analysis, Polling, Facts, Data and Journalism, September 14, 2016. accessed December 10, 2016, http://kff.org/health-costs/report/2016-employer-health-benefits-survey/.

High-deductible plans provide lower monthly premiums, but you cover more of the costs when you need care. By linking an HSA to your plan, you will gain access to a pool of money to help subsidize the higher deductibles. As you pay your monthly premiums, you may choose to contribute toward your HSA as well. Contributions to these programs are tax deductible, and as you pay for health care expenses, any withdrawals are tax-free. Depending on the rules of the institution that manages your HSA, you may be able to invest the funds inside the account. Balances can continue to grow into the future, with no requirement that the money need to be used in the year it was contributed.

FSAs differ from HSAs in this way: FSAs don't need to be linked to a specific health plan. Contributions are still pretax and withdrawals are tax-free, but if you don't use the funds in your FSA in the year they were contributed, you may lose the money. These balances cannot be carried over year-to-year. FSAs can be used for dependent care expenses too. Many people take advantage of these programs as a way of paying for daycares or nanny expenses using pretax dollars.

If you are self-employed, some special deductibility rules often apply to you. You may be able to deduct health insurance premiums for you and your employees as a business expense. You may also be able to deduct any long term care premiums that you cover for the group.

If you're not self-employed but have health care related bills that exceed 10% of your adjusted gross income, you may be able to deduct the amount over the threshold. These expenses may include copays, deductibles, coinsurance amounts, and even premiums. This does not include any reimbursed expenses or bills related to cosmetic procedures. Be sure to speak with a tax professional for more information on how to deduct these expenses.

Medicare

As you get closer to retirement, you'll need to know more about Medicare. Medicare is a government-sponsored program that provides health insurance to seniors and disabled individuals. The government created Medicare to help control insurance costs for older Americans because costs for this age group were as much as three times more than that for younger people. Just as with Social Security, American workers pay into the Medicare system, which generates the revenue needed to provide benefits.

Benefits must be elected by 65 years of age; otherwise, a penalty may be imposed. There is a 7-month grace period to qualify for benefits. This begins 3 months before you turn 65, the month you turn 65, and ends 3 months after the month you turn 65. If you or your employed spouse are currently enrolled in a group health insurance plan, you may retain this health coverage and are exempt from the penalty. One word of caution: if you have health coverage from an employer with fewer than 20 workers, check with your plan, as you may still be required to enroll at age 65.

The Medicare system is split into different parts. Many people find the options complex and hard to understand. Choosing the optimal mix of benefits for your situation is important, so make sure to review each section carefully and consult a financial professional for guidance.

• Part A — Hospital & Hospice Insurance

Medicare Part A covers inpatient hospital stays, including semiprivate rooms, food, and tests. This includes hospital visits to treat an acute illness, as well as skilled long-term care for up to 100 days. Hospital stays must be classified as inpatient to be covered under Part A, which is determined by the "Two-Midnight Rule." If a patient needs hospital care that "crosses two midnights," it is "generally appropriate" for Part A to cover this patient. Part A of Medicare also provides hospice benefits for terminally ill individuals with less than six months to live.

• Part B — Medical Insurance

Medicare Part B is similar to individual health insurance because it pays for covered services after a patient has reached his or her deductible. Services covered under Part B include lab tests, surgeries, and doctor visits. It also covers medical supplies, like wheelchairs and walkers, as well as preventive services, like flu shots. There are added premiums for this coverage, but the Medicare program may significantly subsidize these premiums.

- **Part C — Medicare Advantage**

Medicare Part C allows covered individuals to receive their benefits from a private health care plan instead of the federal government. This provides additional features that enhance the benefits under Parts A and B.

For example, the Medicare Advantage plan may add an out-of-pocket maximum, which caps the amount an individual may spend on health care costs under Part B. In addition, the majority of Part C plans include preventive dental care, eye care, hearing assistance, and gym memberships. These plans may also include prescription drug coverage too.

With a Medicare Advantage plan, you can effectively get all Medicare parts in one plan. There is an additional premium for this, but plans can reimburse some or all the Part B premium to offset the cost.

- **Part D - Prescription Drug Plans**

Medicare Part D covers prescription drugs. Since the federal government does not administer Part D plans, private insurance carriers offer plans to Medicare beneficiaries to help offset the cost of prescription drugs. Under this plan, individuals choose which drugs they wish to cover and at what level (or tier) they wish to cover them. Individuals may decide to not cover some drugs at all. There is an additional premium for this part of Medicare coverage.

- **Medigap Coverage**

Medigap covers many of the copays and coinsurance costs related to Medicare-covered services but is offered through a private insurance company. For an extra premium, you can buy Medigap insurance to cover the medical costs that are your responsibility. You can choose from a variety of different benefit levels to help supplement your Medicare plan.

Whatever your political leanings concerning Medicare or health care in general, health insurance is undoubtedly an important piece of your financial puzzle. As you review all the different options available to you, make sure you choose a plan that addresses your specific situation. If you feel overwhelmed when choosing a Medicare plan, reach out to your financial advisor to help you work through the options.

Chapter 11
Tax Planning

In this world, nothing can be said to be certain, except death and taxes.
—Benjamin Franklin

The United States Tax Code is so complex that even those with CPA designations get confused by all the intricacies and nuances. Every few years, tax laws change, and it's hard to keep up with the updates and amendments. That makes it even more important for us to understand the basics, why taxes exist in the first place, and how to avoid potential pitfalls. Keep in mind that every person's tax situation is different, and you should speak to a tax advisor about your specific situation.

Tax Code Basics

While many people have negative views toward the tax system, try to remember the purpose it serves and why taxes are important. Without taxes, we wouldn't have roads, public schools, museums, and libraries. Also, if your house caught on fire or you were robbed, nobody would be around to help you. We also wouldn't have our military to protect us from any outside threats. Our world would look a lot different without taxes.

Even before our country was formed, taxes were prevalent. The American Colonies were subjected to taxation by England and then Great Britain as early as 1634.[35] As far as America's ability to tax its own citizens, the power to tax lay only with the states until the US Constitution was adopted in 1787 and fully ratified in 1790.

At that point, the federal government gained the ability to lay and collect taxes, but only in the form of trade tariffs. The first federal income tax was adopted in 1861; it was highly contested and said to be unconstitutional.[36] Then, in 1913, with ratification of the Sixteenth Amendment, the federal government gained the power to tax both property and labor.

Throughout the 20th century, income taxes fluctuated like a roller coaster. During World War I and World War II, taxes rose sharply. Shortly after each war, taxes fell. Higher taxes were needed to pay for the wars and government programs, while lower taxes were intended to spur economic growth and recovery. Tax rates have been changed 34 of the 97 years between 1913 and 2010, or about every three years.

- **Income Tax**

The federal income tax system is based on a graduated schedule. The more income you earn, the higher tax rate you pay, though income tax filers receive deductions and credits for certain items that the government wants to incentivize.

A deduction reduces the income subjected to tax, whereas a credit reduces the tax itself. This is an important distinction to keep in mind as you're preparing and reviewing your tax return. Some states and local municipalities adopt a similar income tax system, while others

---

[35] Jens P. Jensen, *Property Taxation in the United States*, (Chicago, IL: University of Chicago Press, 1931) (referring to a 1634 Massachusetts property tax statute).

[36] Revenue Act of 1861, Act of August 5, 1861, Chap. XLV, 12 Stat. 292 (Aug. 5, 1861).

simply use a flat tax rate. A handful of states do not impose a state income tax altogether.

Each year, you will be issued a document to report the income you earned. If you're an employee, you'll most likely receive a W2 form, showing your taxable income. You may also receive a 1099. This form is used when you have received any consulting income, interest or dividend income, or other forms of non-employee income.

- **Capital Gains Taxes**

Capital gains taxes are another form of tax, imposed on profits made from purchased assets. The most common form of these taxes are those paid on stocks, bonds, and mutual funds.

To calculate your capital gains taxes, it's important to know your cost basis. This is the portion of the asset that you've invested and have already paid taxes on. When you sell the asset, you subtract the cost basis from the sale price to get the capital gain. If you sell the asset for less than your cost basis, then you are said to have a capital loss.

Some capital gains may receive preferential tax treatment over ordinary income taxes. As long as you hold the asset for longer than one year, you'll be able to qualify for long-term capital gains rates, which can be significantly lower than short-term capital gains tax rates.

If your house is the asset in question, you may qualify for a significant exemption on the capital gains susceptible to taxation. If you've lived in the property for two of the last five years, then you and your spouse can use this exemption to avoid paying capital gains tax once you sell.

If you end up selling an asset for a loss, then you may be able to use the amount of the loss to offset any capital gains you may have incurred during the same calendar year. If you lack any other capital gains, then you may be able to deduct that loss against your ordinary income taxes. You can deduct up to $3,000 per calendar year, until the total loss has been used up. Keep in mind that a loss on the sale of your personal residence is considered a nondeductible expense and cannot be used to offset any gains.

- **Payroll Taxes**

Another tax that most Americans must pay is the payroll tax. This tax helps to finance government social programs like Social Security, Medicare, and unemployment benefits. These programs are funded by taxing the pay of American workers under the Federal Insurance Contributions Act (FICA). Your payments into the system subsidize those people who are claiming benefits today. As you pay into the system, you earn credits, which entitle you to your own benefits at a later date when you qualify.

- **Sales Taxes**

Sales taxes are another form of tax that you'll encounter. This type of tax is imposed on the sale of certain goods and services. Most merchants collect this tax at point-of-purchase and are required to remit the tax back to the governing body.

Each state imposes its own tax on goods and services purchased in its jurisdiction. The federal government can also impose excise taxes, its form of sales taxes, on both gasoline and cigarettes.

- **Transfer and Estate Taxes**

Another tax you might encounter during your life, as well as at your death, are transfer taxes. If you transfer, or give away, assets during your lifetime that exceed the federal annual exemption, the assets may be subject to a gift tax.

Upon your passing, your estate is tallied up. If these assets exceed a certain threshold, they may be subject to federal, and potentially state, estate taxes.

When you buy or sell a house, you probably will incur transfer and recordation taxes. These go to your state or local municipality as a closing cost, and they cover fees related to retitling and deed filing at your local courthouse.

Tax Planning with Investments

When it comes to your investments, it doesn't matter what you earn, it matters what you keep. If you earn an 8% return on your investment but pay 15% capital gains taxes on your growth, your net return is 6.8%. When you take into account inflation, you might end up with a net real return of a mere 4%.

The impact of real returns can be best illustrated with Certificate of Deposit (CD) rates from 2010–2015. During this time, if you were holding CDs, you actually lost money after taxes and inflation were taken into account. This is why it's so important to invest in tax-advantaged accounts and investment instruments.

Just as it's important to diversify your investment portfolio across many different asset classes, it's also important to diversify across the three different tax buckets: 1099 Now, 1099 Later, and 1099 Never.

- **1099 Now**

1099 Now accounts provide few tax benefits in themselves. Every year that you earn interest, dividends, or capital gains, you are issued a 1099 form to file with your tax return. While these accounts don't contain any inherent tax benefits, they do provide liquidity since you can withdraw the money without penalties. As such, these accounts work well for short-term and mid-term savings goals.

You should consider tax efficient investments inside these accounts, such as municipal bonds, ETFs, and low-turnover mutual funds. These accounts may be eligible for capital gains tax treatment. Brokerage accounts, banks accounts, direct mutual fund, and stock accounts are included within the 1099 Now category.

With these accounts, you could consider employing a Tax Loss Harvesting strategy. This allows investors to "harvest" losses in their portfolio for tax purposes. For example, if you own $12,000 of ABC stock that you purchased for $20,000 and have held for more than one year, you can sell the stock for a loss and realize the $8,000 of capital loss. You can choose to offset any gains in your portfolio with this loss, or you can deduct $3,000 of the loss from your ordinary income and carry forward the remaining $5,000 for future tax years. Be careful of the Wash Sale Rule. If you buy back the same or substantially identical stock within 30 days, you void, or wash-out, the deductibility of the tax loss.

Many people don't like this strategy from a psychological perspective because it means locking in a loss with no chance of recovering. However, you can use the proceeds to buy back a similar security, or wait on the sidelines for more than 30 days and buy the same stock back after the waiting period has expired.

- **1099 Later**

Accounts that fall in the 1099 Later bucket provide for tax deferral on your investment gains. Instead of receiving a 1099 report each year, taxes are deferred until you access the funds in the future. Oftentimes, pretax contributions can fund these accounts, but when you take the money out, you will be subjected to ordinary income taxes.

While tax deferral of gains and tax deductibility of contributions are huge advantages, these accounts generally include a penalty for withdrawals before you reach age 59 ½. As a result, consider using these types of accounts for longer-term goals, such as retirement. 1099 Later accounts include 401(k)s, traditional IRAs, and annuities.

- **1099 Never**

Accounts within the 1099 Never bucket provide similar tax deferral as 1099 Later accounts, but if you meet certain requirements, you may be able to access the funds in the future completely tax-free. This is a huge advantage for a taxpayer who wants to build growth inside an account without the worry of a big tax bill in the future. Since these accounts follow set rules on what is considered a qualified withdrawal, be careful to use these accounts for their designated purpose, so you won't jeopardize the potential tax benefits in the future.

For example, you wouldn't want to save for a boat using a 529 College Savings Plan since you would be taxed and penalized on the growth. Likewise, you wouldn't want to buy a house with Roth IRAs or Health Savings Accounts (HSAs). To qualify for tax-free withdrawals, be sure to use those accounts for retirement and health expenses respectively.

Life insurance cash values would fall into this category as well, but you can access these funds with far fewer limitations. Loans and withdrawals may create an adverse tax result in the event of a lapse or policy surrender and will reduce both the cash value and death benefit. These accounts can be used to fund a variety of different goals throughout a person's lifetime.

Time Horizon	Account Types
Long-Term Goals Retirement, Boat, Vacation Home	401(k)s, IRAs, Roth IRAs, Cash Value Life Insurance, Annuities, HSAs
Mid-Term Goals College, House, Car	Brokerage Accounts, Cash Value Life Insurnace, 529 College Savings Plans
Short-Term Goals Emergency Savings, Vacation, House	Checking, Savings, Money Markets, Certficates of Deposit

Each one of these accounts has their place in an investment plan. It's important to match short-, mid-, and long-term goals with the appropriate types of accounts. While you may be able to access the funds in a long-term account for an earlier need, it's not typically advised to use them for the wrong reasons.

For example, a 35-year-old would not want to use an IRA to buy a car or use a bank savings account to save for retirement. Just because you *can* do it doesn't mean it's the most effective strategy to maximize your tax benefits.

Tax Myths

Since the US Tax Code is so complex, you may encounter myths and misinformation that lead you astray as you make financial decisions. It's important to understand the truth behind these myths so you can achieve your financial goals effectively.

- **Owing Money at Tax Time Is Bad**

The first prevalent myth relates to filing your annual tax return. Many people believe that owing money on your tax return is a bad thing. After all, you've been paying throughout the year and now the government wants to come in and take even more money from you.

Filing your tax return each year is merely a reconciliation of your tax bill. Imagine that you owe your uncle $100 by the end of the year. If you pay him $8 per month, at the end of the year, he will say that you still owe him $4. The amount that you owe to Uncle Sam hasn't changed, you just didn't pay it during the year.

Many people prefer paying taxes as they earn their paychecks throughout the year. On the W4 Tax Withholding form that you file with your HR department, you choose the number of exemptions you'd like to claim. The lower the number, the greater the withholding. Keep in mind that if you elect too many exemptions and not enough tax is withheld, you may be penalized for under-withholding.

If you're a business owner without a formal payroll system, you may choose to file quarterly estimates instead. Since business revenue can be variable, you file these estimates based on your best guess of expected income. Whether you're a business owner or not, ideally you'll want to withhold enough money throughout the year so that, come April 15, you don't owe too much or get refunded too much.

- ## Getting a Large Tax Refund Is Good

On the flip side, you may withhold too much money. Some people use their withholdings as a forced savings strategy. You may send more than enough to the IRS through your tax withholdings so that you receive a large refund to be used for a vacation or a major purchase each year.

This strategy has a few big drawbacks. While the IRS will penalize you for under-withholding, they will not credit you any interest for over-withholding. Furthermore, money sent to the IRS cannot be refunded to you throughout the year. You'll have to wait until you file your return in April to access the funds. So if you fall on hard times and need some of the money back, you won't be able to access it.

As an alternative strategy for saving money, you could set up an automatic deduction from your checking account to your savings account. You may also do this by splitting your direct deposit into two accounts. This will give you the automatic savings strategy you need while keeping the money liquid and potentially earning some interest.

- ## Earning More Money Changes Your Tax Rate

Some people have the luxury of earning variable income, where the harder or smarter they work, the more money they make. This could be someone in sales who works on commission, someone with an incentive or bonus pay, or almost any business owner. Some of these individuals believe that if they earn more money, it will place them in a higher tax bracket, jeopardizing the lower tax rate they have now.

In reality, you may end up paying higher taxes on the higher amounts that you earn, but this doesn't magically change the tax rate applied to the rest of your income. Since federal income taxes are graduated, you pay lower tax rates on the lower portions of your income, and higher rates as you go up the scale. If you end up crossing over into a new tax bracket, only the amount that has crossed over each threshold will be subjected to each higher tax rate.

Let's look at an example of how the federal income tax system works using graduated tax brackets. Samantha earns $60,000 of taxable income and wants to know how much tax she will owe. The first $20,000 will be taxed at 10% and the next $40,000 at 15%. Her effective tax rate in this example would be 13.33%, but her income places her in the 15% marginal tax bracket. This means that any more income she earns this year would be taxed at 15%, up to the top of the bracket. Once she crosses over to the next bracket, then only the income that falls over the threshold will be taxed at the next rate.

• Deductions = Free Money

It is true that the more you deduct from your tax return, the fewer taxes you owe. At the same time, you'll need to consider what it takes to receive those deductions and if they are ultimately worth the cost. Certainly, some deductions everyone can take, such as the standard tax deduction, but oftentimes deductions come at a price.

If you're a business owner or have any consulting income, you can deduct unreimbursed business-related expenses. Be careful about spending money on needless expenses only to receive a deduction. Even though you can claim a deduction, you still have to pay for the item you're deducting.

For example, it costs you $500 for a new laptop that you can deduct as a business expense. The deduction provides a reduction of your taxable income by $500. Between federal, state, and local taxes, you could perhaps save 33% by deducting it; however, you still have to pay $500 for the laptop. Think of deductions like a discount. Instead of paying $500 for the laptop, it only cost $335 since you got it for 33% off.

This scenario doesn't impact only business owners. Many Americans deduct mortgage payments, charitable gifts, and retirement plan contributions. While these deductions are helpful, think about what it costs you to receive that deduction.

Tax advisors suggest that you contribute to a retirement plan to receive a deduction. Instead of owing $5,000 at tax time, you can contribute $15,000 to a retirement account, which may then eliminate your tax bill. Even though you save $5,000 in taxes, it costs you $15,000 out of pocket. Although you are paying yourself versus owing Uncle Sam, shifting $15,000 out of liquid cash reserves into your retirement account may take money away from your emergency funds and jeopardize your short-term savings goals.

Nobody likes paying taxes. At the same time, we understand that we do have to pay into the system to reap the benefits of living in a country that provides the services the US does. If we can get past the political rhetoric and begin to take ownership in learning about the basics of our tax system, that will put us on a path to maximizing all our available opportunities and resources to improve our financial position.

This is a case where ignorance is not bliss and could end up costing you a great deal of money. Be sure to work with a tax advisor to help you understand your specific situation. Going at it alone may save you a couple dollars in fees, but you may be missing out on opportunities in the long run. Use a tax advisor whom you trust and that you feel confident will give you the sense that your taxes have been organized and reviewed by a professional.

Chapter 12
Estate Planning

And in the end it's not the years in your life that count.
It's the life in your years.
—Abraham Lincoln

Many people feel that estate planning is only for the wealthy. After all, you probably need to have an estate big enough to require a plan. While you may or may not have millions of dollars in the bank, what goes into your own estate might surprise you. If you combine all your investment accounts, real estate, personal property, life insurance death benefits, and the value of any business entities that you own, it could add up to a sizable amount.

Estate planning essentially coordinates the disbursement of these assets to your heirs according to your desires. Also, it eliminates any confusion related to guardianship for minor or disabled children, which can be mishandled in the absence of written instructions. It also accounts for decisions that need to be made during your lifetime. For example, if you are unable to make financial or health care choices for yourself, you'll want to consider whom to appoint for this important task.

Whether you're a multimillionaire or part of the middle class, set aside some time now to reflect on those end of life decisions and determine who would be the best person to carry out your wishes. To understand why these decisions are so essential, let's review how an estate is typically settled. As said before, this information should not be considered tax or legal advice. You should consult your tax and legal advisor about your specific situation.

Settling an Estate

Many factors go into settling an estate once someone passes away. All the assets are itemized, along with the liabilities and creditors owed money. An estate tax return is prepared, and any taxes owed are paid. Estate taxes may be assessed at the federal and the state level, and those will need to be paid as well.

Each person is entitled to a certain amount of assets exempt from this tax. Any amount over this threshold may be subject to federal, and potentially state, estate taxes. As with many taxes, the estate tax exemption changes each year, and every state has their own set of rules that apply to residents. This is one major factor in determining where to live when you retire.

After all taxes and creditors have been paid and the estate has been reconciled, any leftover assets that haven't been transferred pass to the appropriate people or organizations. The instructions in the deceased's will determine these transfers. This process, called probate, is where the will is "proved" in a court and accepted as a valid legal document. At that time, an executor is named who will be responsible for ensuring the deceased's wishes are carried out.

Creating your own will gives you control over the disposition of your assets and personal effects. If you neglect to create this document, you are said to have died intestate, and the state you live in determines what happens to your assets. The instructions provided by law in the state may not be aligned with your priorities, so creating your own will is important to ensure everything is handled in the way you want.

Probate is a public process, with legal fees and procedures, that often takes months to adjudicate. Some people try to avoid this process so they might expedite the transfer of assets and protect their family's private financial matters. There are four major ways to transfer property outside of probate.

- **Joint Property**

Owning property jointly with a spouse or an heir may be a great way to transfer ownership upon death. Since these assets are titled with multiple owners, they pass directly to the surviving owner or their heirs. There are many types of joint ownership of assets. To avoid probate, set up ownership as Joint Tenants with Rights of Survivorship (JTWROS). Under JTWROS, assets pass directly to the living owner as quickly as administratively feasible. To release funds typically requires a death certificate and new account paperwork.

Before titling property in this fashion, you'll want to review some considerations. First, assets are considered jointly owned, and each owner has an equal, undivided interest in the whole property. Additionally, when assets are titled jointly, there may be some unforeseen tax consequences. For example, if a parent places their child as a joint tenant, they are often unaware that they have made a gift of one-half of the value of the property. If this amount exceeds the annual gift exclusion, there may be tax consequences.

As a bonus for purchasing this book, you have access to the Death of a Loved One Checklist. This will give you clear instructions on what to do after a loved one passes and can give you space to grieve. Download that worksheet at **www.bit.ly/fppbookbonus.**

- **Beneficiary Designations**

Assets like 401(k)s, IRAs, and life insurance policies all have beneficiary designations. By carefully crafting these elections, you can ensure that the funds will pass directly to the intended people or organizations and avoid the probate process. If you have any brokerage accounts without a beneficiary named, consider using the Transfer on Death election (TOD). These provisions add a beneficiary to either a single or jointly titled brokerage account.

Consider reviewing your beneficiary elections at least once a year to ensure they are current and represent your wishes at that time. You can update your beneficiaries by simply filling out a short form. If you have accounts at many different financial institutions, it can get administratively cumbersome. Consider consolidating everything under one roof for easier account maintenance, and select a trusted advisor that your family can meet with when it's time to transition the estate.

- **Trusts**

Many people view trusts as complex instruments that may not be needed for their simple financial situation. While trusts can be used to help manage complicated estates, they can be straightforward too. A trust is simply a relationship where property is held by one party for the benefit of another. The primary reason to create a trust is for control.

There are two types of trusts you may want to consider. Revocable trusts are used during your lifetime to manage assets and control the dispersion of those assets upon your death. Assets can be placed in trust and taken back out, depending on the wishes of the trustee.

During your lifetime, you are the trustee of your own revocable trust, allowing you to make financial decisions as you would if the account was titled in your own name. Upon your passing, your named beneficiaries will receive the assets.

The benefit of forming a trust is that you can impose specific rules to determine how the assets will be transferred. A common provision is one based on age, where 33% of the assets are transferred when a beneficiary turns 25 years old, 50% at 30 years old, and the rest at 35 years old.

Irrevocable trusts are mainly used for estate and tax considerations. Up until now, each of the ways that you can bypass probate do not avoid estate taxes. By placing assets into an irrevocable trust, you are said to be gifting those assets away to the trust, and therefore excluding them from your gross estate.

Individuals often use irrevocable life insurance trusts (ILIT) to hold life insurance policies for tax purposes, so the death benefits will not count in their gross estate. Premium dollars are contributed to the trust and paid to the policy to maintain the contract. The trustee who managed this process must notify the beneficiaries annually that they are entitled to the dollars contributed to pay the premium under a process known as a Crummey Notice. This is an important step that ensures that the trust assets won't be included in your gross estate.

A spousal limited access trust (SLAT) can make a traditional ILIT more flexible by allowing withdrawals for the health, education, maintenance, or support (HEMS) of your spouse. It's important to note that each spouse can have this provision for the benefit of the other. This can be a great tool to access the funds during your lifetime while still having the value of the trust held outside your estate.

The SLAT provision is most relevant when you hold cash value life insurance inside the trust. The cash value of the policy has the potential to grow with some major tax advantages and can be used during your lifetime, all while having the policy held outside your estate. This strategy assumes that withdrawals are made on behalf of your spouse, so if you and your spouse divorce, it could put a wrinkle in your plans. Also, loans and withdrawals may reduce the policy's death benefit and cash value, and could cause it to lapse.

- **Lifetime Gifts**

Another way to transfer property to heirs without going through probate is to make gifts to your heirs during your lifetime. Since any gift you make reduces the value of your estate, this can also reduce or even eliminate estate taxes. Gifts can be in many different forms. Some people like to give away personal items that have monetary and sentimental value. Jewelry is a classic example. You may also want to give gifts of cash to a loved one.

Some people have highly appreciated stock they want to gift. Gifting this asset to charity produces a double dose of tax benefits. You'll receive a tax deduction for the charitable contribution plus you'll avoid paying tax on your unrealized capital gains. Since the charitable organization is a not-for-profit and in a 0% tax bracket, they can sell the shares you gave them and pay no tax.

Each year, you and your spouse may give up to the annual gift exclusion without the need to file a gift tax return. If you make a gift over this threshold, you may need to use your lifetime gift exclusion. Keep in mind that this can impact the amount you're able to exclude from estate taxes at your death.

If you're a small business owner, you may want to gift the shares of your business to your family as part of your succession plan. Creating Family Limited Partnerships (FLPs) may help transfer the shares without losing control of the business. This can be a complex strategy to execute, so consider retaining a financial advisor, tax advisor, and attorney.

Important Documents

As you create your estate plan, you'll want to add a few other documents that provide instructions during your lifetime rather than at or after your death. While your will is often considered the backbone of your estate plan, a living will, also known as an advance medical directive, is essential in spelling out your health care wishes. If at any point you're unable to communicate what you want, due to a coma or other incapacity, a living will allows your family and physicians to follow your own personal choices.

Along with the living will, you may want to appoint an attorney-in-fact or "surrogate" to make healthcare decisions on your behalf. This person may be responsible for interpreting your living will and is someone you authorize to make health care decisions for you. You can limit the authority of your surrogate. They may be authorized to decide only whether a medical treatment will unnecessarily prolong life or be necessary to relieve pain. It's important to choose someone who understands your wishes and whom you trust will abide by them.

Similar to the health care surrogate, a financial power of attorney names a person responsible for making financial decisions on your behalf. Whether they sign legal documents, manage your investments, or simply pay the bills, this person will act as a fiduciary and help you manage the financial household.

If you suffer an incapacity, and can no longer make decisions on your own, these powers must be "durable" to continue. If you would like these powers in force only after an incapacity, you execute a "springing" power of attorney.

After you have worked with an attorney to create your legal documents and feel satisfied with your appointments, you may want to consider drawing up an ethical will. This document conveys your ethical values to your heirs. It often takes the form of a letter to your loved ones and can include family history and stories, cultural and spiritual values, expressions of love, wisdom gleaned from life experiences, requests for forgiveness, the meaning behind family heirlooms, and so forth.

If you have a great deal of information to convey and want to put something together to preserve your legacy, consider writing an ethical will. The simple act of creating the document will bring you a newfound appreciation for your place in the universe.

As you look to create your estate plan, be sure to seek out legal counsel for help. While there are many online programs and software that can help you set up your documents, you'll want to speak to a professional to be sure that your wishes are recorded appropriately.

By completing your estate plan, you will have made important financial and healthcare decisions for yourself and your family. Assets can be transferred with ease and taxes can be paid timely. You will be able to rest easy knowing that a plan is in place and your wishes will be carried out if something bad were to happen.

Chapter 13
Business Planning

I've never felt like I was in the cookie business. I've always been in a feel good feeling business. My job is to sell joy. My job is to sell happiness. My job is to sell an experience.
—*Debbi Fields*

According to the US Small Business Administration, there are 28 million small businesses that account for 55% of all jobs in our country.[37] Despite popular belief, the small business sector is growing rapidly. While corporate America has been downsizing, the rate of small business formation has grown. There has been a decline in the rate of small business failures as well. It's never been a better time to be a small business owner.

Whether you're in the startup phase or have already built a booming enterprise, it's important to understand the variety of financial implications of business ownership. Many people view their small business as an extension of themselves. They have put time,

---

[37] "Small Business Trends | The U.S. Small Business Administration | SBA.gov," Small Business Trends | The U.S. Small Business Administration | SBA.gov, accessed December 09, 2016, https://www.sba.gov/managing-business/running-business/energy-efficiency/sustainable-business-practices/small-business-trends.

energy, and heart into launching the business and want to ensure that it's handled properly.

From entity formation to employee benefits to exit and contingency planning, you must consider many areas to protect, grow, and transition your venture and leave a lasting legacy. It's just as important to work inside your business, generating value to your customers, as it is to work on your business, properly planning for your biggest asset. Set aside time to review the business at a high level and make sure you're maximizing all your opportunities.

Business Formation

Many business owners start with an idea. Whether you want to build a better mousetrap, sell a service, or become a franchise, you'll need to decide what type of business structure to set up. A variety of factors go into this decision, so make sure you weigh all your options.

- **Sole Proprietorships**

As a sole proprietor, you are your own company and are responsible for its assets and liabilities. You don't need to take any formal action to form a sole proprietorship. You simply start selling your products or services, and you're in business. Some common businesses that may work best structured as sole proprietors include consulting, accounting, freelance writing, landscaping, tutoring, or home-based businesses.

The revenue you earn can be offset by businesses expenses to result in a net profit that is taxed as income on your return. Typically, if you're a sole proprietor, you'd complete a Schedule C form to show the profit or loss from your business. If you purchase assets or take on debt, you'll want to factor this into your financial statements as well. Since a sole proprietorship is so simple and cost-effective to create, it's the most popular type of business formed.

- **Partnerships**

When two or more people share ownership of a business, they form a partnership. Each partner contributes to all aspects of the business, including money, property, labor, and skill. In return, each partner shares in the profits and losses of the business.

Since there are multiple decision makers, it's important to discuss a variety of issues up front and develop a legal partnership agreement. The agreement should address major items such as decision-making procedures, the division of profits, dispute resolution, buy-out arrangements, and dissolution of the partnership. Although the law does not require partnership agreements, they are strongly recommended; it is considered extremely risky to operate without one.

To form a partnership, you must register your business with the state. You'll want to register with the IRS to receive your tax identification number and obtain necessary licenses or permits before conducting business. A partnership must file an annual informational tax return to report the income, deductions, gains, and losses from the business's operations. The business itself does not pay income tax but instead passes profits and losses to its partners through a Schedule K-1 form.

- **Corporations**

Owners form a corporation to create a company that is separate and distinct from themselves. With a sole proprietorship or a partnership, the owners are legally liable for the actions and debts of the business. Forming a corporation distances the owners from this liability and helps ensure that losses incurred are limited to the extent of the investment made. To form this entity, you'll need to create articles of incorporation, along with corporate bylaws and statutes. Be sure to properly file these documents with the state.

There are three main types of corporations, each with their own special provisions. With a traditional corporation (C Corp), revenue generated by the business is taxed at a corporate tax rate. After all taxes and expenses are paid, the corporation can choose to retain the profits or pay the profits out to the owners. When owners receive these profits, they may be subject to taxation again at the individual level. While this double taxation is a major disadvantage of a C Corp, the ability to reinvest profits into the company at a lower corporate tax rate is an advantage.

Filing your corporation with a subchapter S classification (S Corp) can be a good alternative to a C Corp. The S Corp provides the same protection from personal liability as a C Corp, yet profits and losses pass through to the owner's individual tax returns, preventing double taxation. This offers a small business the benefit of incorporating, without a major tax burden.

Like C Corps and S Corps, Limited Liability Companies (LLCs) provide liability protection to owners. In addition, LLCs are taxed similarly to S Corps and partnerships, where profits are passed through to the owner's individual tax return. While LLCs seem similar to S Corps, they also differ in several ways.

LLCs are easy to setup and maintain, which can decrease accounting and attorney fees associated with S Corps. There are also fewer restrictions of ownership of LLCs with an unlimited number of potential owners.

At the same time, S Corps may have preferable self-employment tax treatment. This is because owners can be treated as employees and paid a reasonable salary. Finally, LLCs do have limitations on transfer of ownership. All owners must approve the sale of the other owner's shares.

Usually, little thought is given to minimizing taxes when people first start a business since there's little income to be taxed. But, forming the business using the wrong structure can potentially double the tax bill due when it comes time to sell. Work with an attorney and accountant to go over all the ramifications of the election you make in setting up your business, not just today but in the future, as you grow and ultimately transition out of the business.

Retirement Plans

Once your business is up and running, you may start to think about hiring employees. Along with this decision, many business owners begin to review employee benefit options. Employee benefits will help attract and retain good employees, so selecting the right suite of benefits for your company is critical to your future growth and success.

Many companies start by adding a retirement plan to help themselves and their employees save for this critical time. A wide variety of plans may fit the unique needs of your company, so you'll want to review each option before making your decision.

- **401(k) Plans**

Many people see the 401(k) as the default retirement plan option. These plans usually carry the highest administrative and maintenance costs, so make sure to factor this in as you evaluate your options. If you have over 10-15 employees to spread the costs across, a 401(k) might be a good choice. Keep in mind that in creating this type of plan, you may take on an extra fiduciary responsibility.

Traditionally, the 401(k) plan has multiple parties. These include the following: the company needing the plan (or plan sponsor), the employees in the plan (or plan participants), the plan provider, a registered representative who sold and will service the plan, and potentially a third-party administrator.

The plan provider is a company that provides the platform for the plan. You can choose from many different types of plan providers, so you should interview each carefully to find one that fits your company's unique needs. Most platforms come with online access for participants as well.

The third-party administrator keeps the records and reports related to the plan. They are responsible for completing the required documentation to send to the IRS. As the business owner, you may decide to perform some of these functions on your own. If you choose to do this, then you take on the fiduciary responsibility. Or you can share the fiduciary responsibility with another company more specialized to handle these responsibilities.

An investment advisor may be another party to the 401(k) plan. The advisor will help select the right plan to fit your company's needs. They can also help recommend appropriate investment choices for the plan. After everyone agrees on the investment array, the advisor provides education for the participants to help them determine their risk profile.

As you design your 401(k) plan, you can elect to customize a number of provisions to fit your organization. Some plans have a set match percentage based on employee contributions, while others have a discretionary match that can change each year. Along with this, you'll want to define your plan's vesting schedule. Depending on demand amongst your staff, you can add a Roth feature to the plan as well.

- **SIMPLE IRAs**

If your organization consists of less than 10-15 employees, the 401(k) plan may not be cost effective. Instead, you might want to consider the SIMPLE (Savings Incentive Match Plan for Employees) IRA. You can setup and administer these plans easily, as the acronym suggests, and can have minimal cost to the company. These plans allow you to establish a retirement program where each participant can enroll by opening his or her own IRA.

While the plan may be simple to put in place, you should consider how it differs from the traditional 401(k) plans. For example, the matching choices are somewhat limited with a SIMPLE plan. You can choose either a defined 2% salary match, regardless of the employee contributions, or you can match employee contributions, dollar for dollar, up to 3% of salary.

One other point to note is that all deferrals are fully vested. Any time an employee leaves, that employee is entitled to 100% of the plan balance. The maximum annual contributions for these accounts are generally lower than the amount a participant can put away in a 401(k) plan. You'll need to weigh all these factors, along with the plan's administrative simplicity, as you select the best plan for your company.

- **Simplified Employee Pension (SEP IRA)**

For businesses with few or no employees, a Simplified Employee Pension (SEP IRA) may make the most sense. SEPs allow business owners to defer money for the benefit of themselves and their employees. Employers can put away as much as 20% of net Schedule C income. One caveat with this is that you'll have to contribute the same percentage to all other employee's accounts as well.

SEPs cannot support employee deferrals, so if employees want to contribute their own money, they will need to set up separate plans. You can open these types of accounts any time before your tax filing deadline. As a result, your tax advisor might recommend you set one up to potentially lower the taxes you owe.

- **Solo 401(k)**

Also known as an individual 401(k), the solo 401(k) is designed for business owners with no employees, other than their spouse. This plan has similar features as the SEP IRA and a 401(k), since the company can make the same employer-side contributions as with the SEP, and the participant can defer additional amounts up to the 401(k) contribution limits.

Similar to the SEP, contributions made by the employer to the solo 401(k) must be done for all participants. Like a 401(k), Roth provisions may be added, and loans can be granted as well. Solo 401(k) accounts must be setup prior to December 31, so you won't be able to do last minute tax planning with these accounts.

Executive Compensation

Many retirement plans that companies set up for their employees are subject to the Employee Retirement Income Security Act of 1974 (ERISA). This law created many rules and regulations for the retirement planning industry to ensure consumer protection.

As part of ERISA, retirement plans receive their tax benefits that we know and love. At the same time, they must be offered to all eligible participants. This poses a challenge for some employers who might want to offer extra benefits only for their key executives. If an employer were to offer these extra plans, that employer would fall outside of ERISA's scope, losing the major tax advantages in the process.

These plans, called nonqualified deferred compensation (NQDC), grant a select group of people, usually key employees, the ability to defer a percentage of their pay until they leave the job. Key employees must be either highly compensated employees or management. This strategy allows key employees to reduce their current taxable income and in return the employer promises to pay benefits in the future.

You will want to consider several factors before setting up these types of programs. First, the funds set aside for the executive's benefit are subject to the creditors of the company. Also, you'll want to be careful what vehicle you choose to fund the plans. Since the plan itself doesn't provide any tax benefits, any growth inside the account may be subject to tax.

Consider funding these plans using a tax-deferred vehicle, like an annuity or cash value life insurance, since both account types offer big tax benefits. While these plans provide many benefits to employees, they offer some advantages for the employer too.

Companies will win huge brownie points with their key executives for carving out this exclusive benefit just for them. This helps with employee morale, as well as attracting and retaining high-quality people.

Additionally, the company may tie these funds to certain previously agreed-upon eligibility and vesting conditions. This further helps retain executive employees, because they could forfeit the money if they left before achieving the benchmarks. Life insurance is commonly used to fund these plans. If the executive were to pass away, the life insurance proceeds would go to the company.

A life insurance policy informally funding the NQDC plan is subject to the notice and consent rules for employer-owned life insurance (EOLI). Failure to follow those rules will subject any death benefit paid to the employer to income tax.

The primary reason to purchase a life insurance product is for the death benefit. Life insurance products contain fees, such as mortality and expense charges, and may contain restrictions, such as surrender periods.

Exit & Transition

So, you've built your business, provided value to countless customers and employees, and have now reached a stage in your career where you're thinking about your transition out. Whether it's a voluntary retirement or an unplanned death or disability, creating your exit strategy is vital to keeping your legacy alive. Here are five steps toward creating that strategy and ensuring that your wishes are carried out.

- **Set Exit Objectives & Goals**

Many small business owners do not set specific exit and succession objectives. While it can be an emotional process, it's important that your goals are thoroughly contemplated and committed to paper. By answering three straightforward exit-related questions, you will cut through a lot of muddled thinking that otherwise might bar you from moving forward.

1. How much longer do I want to work in the business before retiring or moving on?

2. What is the annual after-tax income I want during retirement (in today's dollars)?

3. To whom do I want to transfer the business?

No owner can effectively begin planning to leave their business without answering each of these questions. You may want to consider other factors that could impact your exit strategy, such as maintaining family harmony, providing for one or more employees, transferring wealth to family members, getting maximum value for the business, as well as any charitable aspirations that you may have.

• Quantify Available Resources

As small business owners transition away from their company, one main objective is securing a retirement income stream. This income will support you and your family's future lifestyle. Pursuing your personal financial goals depends on converting that asset to cash. To ensure that you can generate the needed income from the sale of your business, you must first know its value.

Owners employ several tax-minimizing techniques as they work toward their exits from the business. Consider that, at best, it takes years to reap the benefits of most tax-planning strategies, so be sure to manage expectations accordingly.

• Sale to a Third Party

Owners have a variety of ways to market a business for sale. If your company is worth at least $5 million, you can have an investment banking firm orchestrate a competitive or controlled auction to ensure you receive top dollar for your company. In a competitive auction, multiple qualified buyers come to the negotiating table at the same time, all with the same information, and all prepared to make an offer for the company. This process helps to maximize your leverage and enables you to select the sales price and deal structure; it will also allow you to gauge which buyer's operating philosophy best aligns with your goals and objectives.

If your company is worth less than $5 million, you might still retain an investment banker to perform a competitive auction. More likely, you will use the services of a business broker to engage in a negotiated sale. Typically, a buyer with a high level of interest in purchasing the company will initiate the sale. Although you forgo multiple offers, this process can be more efficient.

• **Transfer to Insiders**

Instead of selling your business on the open market, you may decide to transition ownership interests to people you already know. These individuals could be co-owners, family members, or key employees. As you choose a mechanism to transfer the business, consider one that minimizes both your income tax consequences and your risk of not being paid the entire value of the business.

One way of achieving this is to stay in control until you receive the entire amount of the purchase price. You can create an installment sale where payments are received over an extended period of time. You can also create unfunded obligations from the business long before the actual transfer. These obligations may include nonqualified deferred compensation, leasing obligations, indemnification fees, licensing and royalty fees, and subchapter S dividends.

Contingency Planning

One of the benefits of developing an exit strategy is planning for contingencies. Taking prudent measures so that your business continues if you don't is a natural part of the planning process. You'll want to create a plan for your business upon your death or incapacity. To do this, consider using a buy-sell agreement. Think of this document as a business will that spells out what will happen to the company in the event of the death or disability of an owner or partner.

Since a plan is only as good as its execution, be sure to fund these obligations with life and disability insurance. This will help ensure that your wishes can be carried out and that cash is available to facilitate the plan. Don't forget to review these plans every few years to confirm that they follow new business valuation models.

Financial Planning for Business Owners

Small business owners have a unique wrinkle in their financial plans. Not only will you need to create a strategy for your family and household finances, but also one for your business. Many business owners create business plans for their company, but some forget to create financial plans.

The business financial plan should be a comprehensive review of where the company is today, the exit strategy for the owners, and all the factors to consider along the way. From employee benefits to executive compensation and key employee protection, reviewing these items will help the company maintain its growth path and protect itself from challenges that could derail that trajectory.

If you're a small business owner without employees, you may not need to create a plan for some of these items. Regardless, no matter the size of the business, creating a business financial plan will help you answer many logistical questions and fine-tune the business's role in your own personal financial picture.

Some common items you can address with your financial planner include estimated tax payments, living on variable income, business bank accounts and budgets, and paying yourself a salary versus taking distributions. Ultimately, you want to integrate your business finances with your personal finances to maximize opportunities and avoid challenges.

Be sure to arm yourself with a trusted team of professionals who can help you manage all these important areas. Your financial planner, tax advisor, and attorney should all coordinate to help you create, implement, and review your plans. Rely on them and their expertise as you navigate toward your goals.

Part 3
Fitting Your Pieces Together

Chapter 14
New Baby Planning

Getting a burp out of your little thing when she needs it is probably the greatest
satisfaction I've come across at this point in my life.
—Brad Pitt

Congratulations! You're having a baby! After the initial excitement has worn off, the preparations begin. You undoubtedly know the difference between all the different types of anti-colic bottles on the market, but you may not have reviewed your finances with the same level scrutiny.

Before the baby is born and diapers and onesies consume your life, take a minute to create a financial plan to support your new bundle of joy. It could save you tons of money and give you a sense of security so you can sleep soundly—when you have time for it again.

Cash Flow & Budgeting

One of the first major steps in planning for your new baby is to create a budget. This helps you and your partner understand the income coming in and expenses going out. Funds for new baby costs will need to come from somewhere. You may decide to forgo some discretionary spending for a little while, like dining out or going to the movies. Alternatively, you may decide to scale back your savings plans for a bit. Either way, it's critical to understand your household cash flow so you can make intelligent choices.

If you and your partner both work, you'll need to have care for your young one. Selecting the right daycare is not only a hard, emotional decision but also a major financial one as well. This is often a family's biggest monthly expense related to the child. Consider opting for the Dependent Care Flexible Spending Account (FSA), if your company has one. This will allow you to contribute pretax dollars to a plan exclusively to pay for childcare expenses. This could save you a substantial amount of money each year.

One of the major discussions parents have is the potential for one parent to stay home with the baby. If you are considering this, take a hard look at your budget to see how your family's lifestyle would be different with only one income. If the stay-at-home parent's income after taxes is not substantial enough to outweigh the costs of childcare, then from a financial standpoint, it might pay to stay at home. If the lost income is significantly more than the costs of childcare, then it might be more financially sound for both parents to work. There are many other factors that go into making these decisions, so contemplate all the variables.

Once you've nailed down your budget, you may want to start socking some money away in your savings account at the bank. This will act as your emergency reserves, in case something catastrophic happens during this time. What would you do if you or your partner lost your job or fell ill, or if your car broke down? This cash pot will be there in case you need it. The last thing you want during this time is added stress.

You might also plan to accumulate this cash to help finance maternity leave. If your company doesn't have a favorable policy, which forces you to take leave without pay, then the cash could be used to help subsidize your lost income during this time.

If your pregnancy ends up going smoothly and you find yourself having too much cash after living on your new budget, then you can decide to reinvest the funds. The right amount to have in this account depends on your situation and your comfort level. Many experts recommend three to six months of expenses, but during this uncertain time in your life, you may want to opt for a bit more.

Insurance Protection

As you ponder what life will be like with a new member of the family, consider reflecting on what that life would be like if you or your partner were no longer around. While it might feel a bit morbid to think about, it's better to run through worst-case-scenarios now and create a plan for them, than to be caught off guard suffering a major financial hardship.

Many people review their financial obligations and create a list of items they'd want to be covered if either parent were to pass away. Statistics show that 86% of consumers don't buy life insurance because it's too expensive and they overestimate the true cost by more than two times.[38] While it is true that life insurance is an added expense to the budget, it's critical in helping ensure that your family's wishes can be carried out.

Money is infused into the household budget when it is needed the most. Debts can be paid off, college accounts can be instantly funded, and income can be replaced. While you or your partner may no longer physically be around to care for your child, the money paid out from a life insurance policy can make a significant impact on how your child grows up. Purchasing life insurance also makes a statement to your family and indirectly teaches your children about the importance of proper risk management.

Beyond life insurance, you may decide to review your disability protection as well. Many companies offer disability insurance coverage

---

[38] *2015 Insurance Barometer Study*, LIMRA, accessed December 09, 2016, http://www.orgcorp.com/wp-content/uploads/2015-Insurance-Barometer.pdf.

as an employee benefit. As we discussed in an earlier chapter, if you cannot work to earn your paycheck due to illness or injury, you may be entitled to a percentage of your salary. Group plans are a great start, but most cap your benefits, and any money received is usually taxable. Additionally, most disability plans won't cover maternity leave, only a complication during your pregnancy.

Reviewing your disability coverage is a good idea to ensure that, if you were no longer able to do your job and bring in a paycheck, that money would be available to cover household expenses. This is especially important if you're a member of a one-income household. Protecting that income is critical to ensuring that the family's financial goals are attainable.

One other aspect of insurance that many new parents review is the family's health insurance plan. Whether you buy your coverage through your employer or another outlet, consider the costs of adding a new baby to the plan. Many insurance carriers give you a limited window of time once the baby is born to add that child to the plan. Make sure you know your insurance company's procedures, and prepare as best as you can. In addition, if provided, consider adding a health care FSA to help pay health care expenses with pretax dollars. Be careful not to put too much into these accounts since some of the money may be lost if you don't use it in the year contributed.

Estate Planning

In conjunction with proper insurance planning, it's also a good idea to create an estate plan. As mentioned in an earlier chapter, even if you lack a substantial net worth, estate planning helps you and your partner discuss important decisions. One of the most relevant items is naming a guardian for your child should you and your partner pass away.

Whether you appoint family or friends, be sure to discuss your intentions with the named individuals and confirm they are okay taking on the responsibility. Consider sharing with them all or a portion of your estate plan so they know that this responsibility does not come with a financial hardship.

Related to this is who to list as beneficiaries on your retirement accounts and life insurance policies. It's generally not a good idea to name a minor as a beneficiary. A good alternative is to name a guardian or a trust for the benefit of the minor. This will allow the money to be used for the child's benefit without giving the child unlimited access the funds for anything they want before the age of majority.

College Funding

Many parents think about opening college accounts for their children when they are born. While we know that the sooner we begin funding the plan, the more money we will save for educational expenses, it makes sense to take a step back and pause for a moment. During the first few months of your new baby's life, you'll experience a lot of financial pressure. Your first priority is to make sure your budget is operating the way you planned before adding another savings strategy to the mix.

Consider starting a college account but leaving it dormant without any monthly contribution for a while. Friends or relatives might want to make a contribution to the plan, so investing any gifts received could help fund the account without impeding your budget. Once you get into a groove and feel comfortable with your new normal, consider adding this account to your savings strategy. Be careful not to forgo your own retirement savings to fund these accounts. Remember, you can always borrow for college, but you can't borrow for your own retirement.

Whatever you end up planning, be sure that you and your partner are on the same page. This is a stressful time in your lives, so discuss your hopes and dreams, as well as your fears and anxieties. If the two of you stand together as a united front, you will be able to push through the good and the bad times. After all, it's good practice as you navigate your newfound roles as parents.

Chapter 15
Teaching Your Kids About Money

All kids need is a little help, a little hope,
and somebody who believes in them.
—*Magic Johnson*

More fundamental than how to solve a quadratic equation or the distance of a light year, personal finance is a core skill that everyone needs to learn. Similar to reading, writing, and the development of language, without knowing how money works and its role in our society, you will struggle to properly take care of yourself and your loved ones.

Kids don't receive even basic personal financial knowledge. Schools are only now teetering on the frontier of providing classes with the fundamental information, but that's not enough. In fact, over half the country scored a *C* or worse on the 2015 National Report Card on State Efforts to Improve Financial Literacy in High Schools, a report produced by the Center for Financial Literacy at Champlain

College in Burlington, VT.[39] The report measures financial education efforts across the U.S.

With or without the support of the public education system, parents need to step in and coach their kids on the pleasures and the dangers of money. Experts agree that parents wield an incredible amount of influence over their children's habits and behaviors. Be *on purpose* about your parenting when it comes to personal finance, and you'll help your kids learn to help themselves.

Preschoolers

One of the best places to start teaching your kids about money is at the grocery store. They'll be able to see you place items in your cart and use money to buy the food and take it home. This is a great context to discuss what money is and why it's important. You can also begin teaching your children why Daddy and/or Mommy go to work every day.

Tell them the story of the dollar in your pocket. The journey that it's been on and who has come in contact with it. If you're lucky, you may have found a "Where's George" bill. This is a dollar bill that has a special stamp on it that tracks its travels. You can look up online all the places it's been and help narrate the story. This will get their imagination going and hold their attention.

At some point, you may want to buy your kids a bank. Instead of opting for the classic "piggy" varieties, choose one with a more practical application. There are a variety of manufacturers that divide the bank into four compartments: Spend, Save, Invest, and Give. As your child places their money in the bank, let them choose the slot to fund and explain the importance of each.

---

[39] "IS YOUR STATE MAKING THE GRADE? 2015 National Report Card," accessed December 09, 2016, http://www.champlain.edu/centers-of-excellence/center-for-financial-literacy/report-making-the-grade.

Elementary Schoolers

As your child grows up, they will inevitably want things. Remind them about their own bank and the choices they make with their money. You may decide to begin an allowance. If you do, make sure to tie the allowance to certain responsibilities around the house. Setting an allowance amount is important as well. Consider splitting the regular amount into four parts so they can put money toward each of their goals.

Another take on an allowance that some parents implement is paying for special projects above and beyond normal household duties, such as cleaning the garage or shoveling snow. Make sure you pay them their money soon after the work is completed. Studies show that the sooner you provide positive reinforcement, the more likely the behavior will be repeated. Also, the amount paid for each project should be equivalent to the work that was completed. If the work was hard or took a long time, consider providing a greater value for that effort.

Aside from hiring your child to do household work, encourage other entrepreneurial avenues. Selling popcorn or cookies through their local scout troop is a great way to teach business skills at an early age. Lemonade stands provide great learning opportunities. Find something your child can be passionate about and let them run with it.

Remember that all work and no play is no fun. Bring in classic board games to help your child learn to accumulate money. Monopoly Jr. and The Game of Life are great starting points. Be careful not to frustrate your child with all the rules. Putting too much pressure on them to learn the game's details might backfire. Consider opting for "house rules" and, as they grow older, change the rules to accommodate their abilities.

Tweens and Teens

During these crucial years, you should teach your children more advanced money lessons. Work with them to open a savings account at the bank and help them fill out the necessary deposit or withdrawal slips. Teach them how the banking system works and the joys of compound interest. Also, cover the basics of checkbooks and credit cards.

In addition, discuss charity and the importance of giving to a good cause, both in the form of money and time. Even if you have little of either to spare, teach your children to recognize what they do have and how even a little bit can go a long way.

As children grow into teenagers, their use of money changes. Help your teenage children practice saving towards a financial goal. Whether they want to buy their own car or the newest video gaming system, this important strategy will help them develop good habits.

This is also a good time to talk about stocks, bonds, and the financial markets overall. If possible, take a field trip to Wall Street and tour the New York Stock Exchange. Tie this in with saving for retirement and the importance of starting early. Consider opening a Roth IRA for your children and match their contributions. You can do this as long as their earned income meets or exceeds the total amount contributed. With these instructions, they can begin building their retirement nest egg, as well as internalize good saving habits.

Young Adults

Oh, the college years. These are the times when your teens become young adults, frivolously racking up credit card debt, digging deeper into student loan debt, and spending their cash on beer and nights out. Parents would do well to step in and guide their collegiate offspring about the importance of managing credit wisely. Since their financial education started early, you may actually head off some of the common problems they may have faced managing debt. You can share stories about others wallowing in debt and being irresponsible about paying it back and how this can jeopardize their chances of one day affording a home.

Once a year, sit down with your son or daughter and review their credit report and FICO score. Discuss the basics of a mortgage and how to obtain one. Finally, cover the risks of foreclosure but also the ultimate emotional and financial satisfaction of homeownership. After graduation and obtaining that first "real" job, help guide them to create a budget and itemize their income and expenses. Share with them ideas on what to do with the leftovers, if any.

Beyond that, always be a resource for your children. Let them create their own lives and meaning of money, but serve as a consultant to answer questions and share experiences. Be a good example for your kids as well. Practice what you preach and share with them, within reason, some of the strategies you are implementing in your plan. Mistakes are inevitable, so be there to help them through it. In the end, if you do your job right, they will live as financially responsible adults and one day will thank you for taking them on the journey of discovering personal finance.

Chapter 16
Millennial Money Management

The most important investment you can make is in yourself.
—Warren Buffett

The Millennial generation is said to be one of the greatest cohorts of people in decades. These individuals, born in the early 1980s–2000, have grown up in the Internet age with instant access to an abundance of information. They aren't afraid to try new things or to fail. They are also leaders of change and idealism. They stay rooted in core values and champion equal rights, all while challenging the status quo.

Some have even compared the Millennial generation to the "Greatest Generation" (those born early in the 20th century). Millennials have suffered the effects of the Great Recession, which continues to affect jobs and other opportunities. As a result, many millennials have become more risk averse with their investing habits.

Research shows that Millennials are postponing marriage, starting families, and even home buying. They cherish their personal freedom more than settling down and choose to spend their money on experiences rather than possessions. As a consequence, they are delaying their financial planning and may be missing out on some major opportunities.

Invest Now!

We've already seen the power of compound interest at work and realize the importance of starting savings plans at an early age. As a consequence, waiting just five years to begin an investment plan can seriously affect a person's ability to reach long-term financial goals. So, what can Millennials do, besides starting early, to increase their chances of achieving financial freedom?

- **Tax-Advantaged Accounts**

For one, Millennials can begin using tax-advantaged ways of saving. Roth accounts are a beneficial resource for those who have many years until retirement. You can withdraw investments inside these accounts tax-free in retirement. Through Roth accounts, Millennials can pay their taxes now so they won't have to later.

A person's anticipated tax bracket in retirement will determine whether a Roth account or a traditional IRA will provide more money in retirement. Generally, investors who will be in a higher tax bracket at retirement (relative to their current tax bracket) benefit more from a Roth account than an investor who is in a lower tax bracket at retirement.

Millennials can use life insurance cash values as an investment tool as well. The cash value in these policies can be accessed tax-free for any reason. But remember that policy loans and withdrawals may create an adverse tax result in the event of a lapse or policy surrender, as well as reduce both the cash value and death benefit. Cash value life insurance and Roth accounts complement each other well since you can use them for different purposes.

The life insurance's main purpose is to protect a dependent in the event of your death. As a Millennial, you might choose to defer this type of product since you might not have any dependents yet. Consider taking another look. By qualifying for life insurance early, while you're young and healthy, you can lock in your policy at potentially better rates. This can benefit you as you grow older if you experience health issues.

- **Invest in Yourself**

Many Millennials come away from college saddled with student debt, which can be a major burden in pursuing financial goals. Reflect on your life situation had you not attended college in the first place. Remember that diploma-holding millennials have annual incomes $17,500 greater than those without a college degree. The cost of education is a great investment since you're making that investment in yourself.

At the same time, some Millennials question whether they could have made a different investment in themselves. With new ideas and big thinking, you may want to start an entrepreneurial venture. Your earlier years may be the best time to explore these opportunities since you don't have other obligations.

In the end, make sure you're doing what you love and live a life without regrets. You only live once (YOLO). Make sure to balance this with a contingency plan. If your new business goes belly up, have a backup plan ready to go. That might take the form of a fallback career, a large emergency reserve, or even support through family and friends.

- **Real Estate**

Buying real estate is one of the first big purchases that a young adult makes. Between the housing market collapse, large student loan payments, and the desire to be nimble in where to call home, Millennials are delaying this investment. There are many pros and cons that go along with this decision, and each has to be weighed carefully.

You can derive some major benefits from owning your own home. Not only is it a big step in realizing the American dream, but it also can have some financial benefits. For one, interest owed on a mortgage may be tax deductible. This could help defray some of the costs of home ownership. Also, if you end up moving out, you may be able to convert the property into a rental with the goal of creating an income-producing asset on your balance sheet.

From an investment standpoint, you can leverage your small down payment into a larger asset. For example, by making a $50,000 down payment on a $250,000 condo, you have effectively leveraged your investment five times. If the value of the condo grows at a hypothetical rate of 2% per year over five years, your house would then be worth $276,000. Assuming you could sell the property for that value, you will have earned a $26,000 gain on only a $50,000 investment. That translates to an 8.74% annualized rate of return over five years, not taking into account any costs associated with the condo.

Yet, this could work the other way, with major losses magnified by that same leverage. Real estate investing could cause you to lose even more than you invested. This happened during the housing market collapse in 2007–2008. That same $250,000 condo could have lost half its value over a short three-year period. You now may be living in a home that's underwater, meaning you owe more to the bank than the value of the house.

Buying a home is a major decision that shouldn't be taken lightly. It can be a good long-term investment if you can ride out market cycles. Be careful to select a home wisely. Consider your time horizon and how this property could be upgraded as you build a family. Being stuck in a property that once suited your needs just fine but later begins to feel small as your family grows is not a good position to be in.

Sometimes renting can provide a lot more flexibility and freedom. With renting, you're not locked into one place and can take on new job opportunities. You also won't be saddled with property taxes and maintenance costs. Plus, you won't have to worry about landlord responsibilities or selling the house if you decide to leave the area. As you make your decision, consider all these factors.

Complications by Friends and Family

Without a doubt, your family and friends significantly impact your finances. After all, they are the most influential people to you and are always there for you when you need them. They can be your biggest advocates as you take on new financial goals and projects, but also can provide big distractions to the success of your plans.

While your friends and family can positively influence your financial plan, be aware of how they can distract you from your goals. As you age and begin a family of your own, you may be asked to become the named guardian of someone else's children. Before accepting this responsibility, consider how this will impact your financial plan. Life happens and doesn't always work out the way we pictured.

Before formally accepting this major responsibility, consider asking about the financial planning steps the parents have taken to provide for the kids if they were no longer around. Is there any life insurance setup? What about a trust? Will they be formalizing their estate plan?

You might want to learn more about why the parents are selecting you over other people. Do they want you to keep the children in the same school system? Do you share similar values? Maybe it's because they think you are more wealthy than you actually are. It's a good idea to know these answers up front so you know how to uphold their wishes if the time ever came.

Another way your financial plan can be impacted by friends and family is through long term care planning for your parents. While it might be awkward at first, it's important for you to know if they have a plan in place for when their health deteriorates. It would be good for you to know if they'd rather have caregivers come to the house or go to a nursing home if care was needed.

In some cultures, it is an honor to physically take care of your parents as they age. While your intentions are honorable, consider the financial implications of being a caregiver. You may need to take time away from work to act in this role or even need to pay out-of-pocket for supplemental skilled care, medications, or equipment. It would be good for you to know all this going in, so you can budget these costs in your plan.

Budgeting and Debt Management

Your budget will be a key resource in helping you make better financial decisions. You'll be able to organize your income sources and expenses in a clear document to help understand where everything is going and how much is left over to save and invest. As it is for most Americans, you might not have much left over. There are a few things you can do to rework your budget to find money to save.

First, review your spending habits. Beyond the traditional brown bag lunch, you can consider eliminating a few other expenses. You might decide to cut the cable cord and watch TV and movies over the Internet through an on-demand streaming provider. While you're at it, get rid of your landline phone too.

Also, consider canceling that gym membership you never use. It might be better to use the equipment at your community clubhouse or simply take a run outside. Finally, it might be worthwhile to review the deductibles on your insurance coverage. Sometimes it pays to increase your deductible to reduce your monthly insurance premium if you're willing to accept more of the risk should you need to use the coverage.

Along with reducing your expenses, you might consider increasing your income. While you might not have much control of your income through your full-time job, you can add a part-time "side hustle" to provide some extra cash. You might decide to become a chauffeur and drive passengers around with the help of your smartphone. If you're artistic, you might choose to sell some of your crafts online in a virtual store. You might even decide to rent out a room in your home.

Whatever you decide to do, remember to balance this part-time work with your social time. Burnout can lead to depression and other emotional challenges. Make sure you choose something fun that will also fit with your work-life balance.

Managing your debt is another place to free up extra money. If you have student loans, consider opting for an income-based repayment program or even a longer payment schedule. Depending on your income level, this strategy could help you manage your monthly payments better and keep you from feeling stuck.

If you work for a not-for-profit agency or the federal government, you may qualify for a public service debt forgiveness program. Be sure to carefully examine the qualifications for these programs because they may be complex.

Some Millennials fall on hard times and use credit cards as a safety net. If you've accumulated some consumer debt, research each card's interest rate and payment terms. List the debts and sort them by highest to lowest rates. Consider making the minimum payments on all the debts and direct any extra funds toward the highest rate card first. As you pay off each card, roll the freed-up cash flow down the list. This will help you pay off your cards faster and save you extra interest payments.

To prevent falling back into debt, build up your cash reserves using an online direct savings account. They can pay higher interest than traditional brick and mortar banks. Also, set aside at least three to six months of expenses for emergencies.

As with anything in life, nothing is certain. As a Millennial, you have many years ahead of you to navigate the world of personal finance, so try new things and see what works for you. You may want to consider hiring a financial planner to help guide you along the way. This is a professional relationship that could last a lifetime, so make sure to do your due diligence. Find a financial planner you feel comfortable with and who understands your unique challenges.

Chapter 17
New Money

Here's something to think about:
How come you never see a headline like "Psychic Wins Lottery"?
—Jay Leno

While it might seem like a far-fetched fantasy, understand that coming into money unexpectedly can be a double-edged sword. Whether you inherit a small fortune, win the lottery, receive a divorce settlement, or win a legal judgment, receiving a large sum of money can be quite intimidating.

Your first instinct might be to go on a shopping spree or a Caribbean cruise. After all, you can't take it with you, right? At the end of the day, you'll need to decide how much of an impact you want this money to have. With a little planning, this newfound money might just be the bolt of lightning to supercharge your financial plan.

Inheritance

As the beneficiary of someone's estate, you may inherit money in a variety of ways. You could receive cash outright. The executor of the estate could send you a check for your portion of the proceeds, and you could simply deposit the funds in your own account. More likely in such a situation, you might receive assets retitled to you. You might collect financial assets or physical property, both of which you can hold as your own, or the revenue from sold assets that you can then direct toward your own financial goals.

If you're the beneficiary of someone else's life insurance policy, you'll want to contact the insurance company as soon as you learn of your loved one's passing. This will start the claims process so you can receive the death benefits as soon as possible. The insurance company will most likely need a copy of the death certificate as well as some completed forms, so come prepared with this information.

A common way you may inherit retirement assets is through a stretch IRA. These IRAs allow the beneficiary to take distributions throughout their lifetime, as opposed to being taxed on the full account balance all at once. This strategy allows the beneficiary to continue to defer taxes on the account balance so the funds can continue to grow.

You may be required to withdraw specified amounts or required minimum distributions each year. You may even decide to use these funds for your own retirement. It's also nice to use this small distribution each year for something special to remember your loved one.

Divorce

You may be in a marital situation that is, unfortunately, ending in divorce. As part of the divorce settlement process, assets are divided between spouses, and funds are disbursed. As you draw up a divorce agreement, you may be entitled to receive a large amount of money from your ex. Be sure to use it wisely.

Often a qualified domestic relations order (QDRO) is used to split retirement accounts. Even though 401(k)s and IRAs follow strict rules on distributions to maintain the tax benefits, QDROs allow for individuals to split assets before retirement age without taxes and penalties. You will need to reinvest these funds in a personal retirement account to preserve the tax benefits.

If you relied on your ex to manage the financial household, you may feel lost, hopeless, and completely overwhelmed by everything. This is certainly an emotional time, so don't go at it alone. Hire a financial professional to work alongside you and help you identify the location and value of everything. This is your new beginning and, as such, a fresh start toward living financially free.

Lottery

So, you finally hit the big one! You're so excited that you jump up and down and scream. It's more money than you've imagined in your wildest dreams. What are you going to do now? Should you quit your job? Go on a shopping spree? Travel the world?

Flash forward six months. The initial euphoria has worn off. What are you going to do now? How will this money change your life? Obviously, you'll want to enjoy the money, perhaps by improving your lifestyle or eliminating financial hardships. At the same time, you know you want to use the money wisely. After paying off your debts, consider stashing most of it away for a rainy day. After all, you'll want this money to last your lifetime, and then some.

Your payout may be offered as a lump sum or in the form of an annuity. If you're a disciplined investor, you may decide to take the lump sum and invest it. If you have some bad spending habits, then you might want to elect the annuity payout to ensure that the money lasts.

As word of your good fortune travels, you may encounter friends or relatives who approach you for financial help. Consider being somewhat altruistic with your newfound wealth, but be careful that these people aren't just using you. As you would help a child, consider helping your loved ones to help themselves. Use the money in such a way that they become better managers of their own finances. The last thing that you want to do is fix their current problems only to find out months later that they're back in the same predicament.

And remember that money matters should be dealt with privately. Be careful with how openly you share your financial situation. While you may trust your friends and family, you never know who might overhear your conversation or let sensitive information slip. Many people fall victim to identity theft or scams that could endanger their newfound wealth. At the same time, don't become paranoid to the point you don't trust anyone. Just make sure that you're an educated consumer and that you've done your homework.

Indemnification of a Loss

You may also receive a financial windfall when you are indemnified for a loss that has occurred. Whether you experienced a major car accident, suffered damage to your home, or were the victim of an assault, you may have received a legal judgment in your favor. Many times these judgments include financial restitution for the loss itself, as well as damages to cover your physical pain, emotional distress, or defamation you experienced.

Whether or not you take legal action, you may end up dealing with an insurance company to indemnify your loss. You've paid your premiums for these policies, and now it's time to file a claim. You'll need to provide appropriate documentation along with your claim to prove your loss and receive the appropriate payout. If you disagree with the amount the company determines they will cover, consider hiring your own legal representative to put pressure on the company to pay the full claim.

Just as with the other types of financial windfalls, be smart with the money you receive. After paying for any damage or expense related to the event, use the money to dig yourself out of other financial hardships you may be currently experiencing and strategize ways to improve your life beyond that point. Consider investing the funds to maximize your payout. Whatever you do, don't fall prey to the temptation to spend it all in one place.

Whether your windfall came from an inheritance, divorce, lottery winning, or settlement, it's important to make smart financial decisions with your newfound wealth. This cash infusion into your financial plan can accelerate you toward achieving your financial goals. Be thoughtful about your plan for the money. You'll be grateful that you were when you've reached your goals and objectives.

Chapter 18
The Modern Family

Family is not an important thing. It's everything.
—Michael J. Fox

The nuclear family sure isn't what it used to be. During the period between 1970 and 2000, our country went through a major shift. In 1970, about 40% of all households contained nuclear families with a father, a mother, and children all under the same roof.[40] When the study was rerun in 2000, the traditional way of creating a family accounted for only about 24% of U.S. households, a 40% reduction. Instead, the number of nontraditional household combinations has risen.

Over the same period, there has been a 150% increase in three other household demographics: (1) households where family members other than the parents raise the children; (2) households represented by single individuals; and (3) divorced families. Since the passing of the 2015 same-sex marriage laws, many more nontraditional families

---

[40] Williams, Brian K., Stacey C. Sawyer, and Carl Wahlstrom. *Marriages, Families, and Intimate Relationships: A Practical Introduction.* Boston, MA: Allyn and Bacon, 2006.

will be created, displacing the nuclear family as the archetype of the American family.

Whether you're a part of a non-traditional family or not, it's important to know how to maximize your financial situation. However, some of the typical financial planning concepts may not apply if you are a part of a nontraditional family. Whether you're a divorcee, in a same-sex household, a late bloomer, have no children, or another nontraditional family situation, there are a variety of ways to fit your financial pieces together to create maximum efficiency.

Divorced Families

Divorce can come with some big emotional and financial scars. Divorces often accompany hefty attorney's fees and contentious conversations. In the midst of the emotional turmoil, it's important to understand the ramifications of a divorce so you can ensure your financial situation is optimized.

The first place to start for many divorcees is creating and understanding your household budget. While it seems pretty basic, it's important to understand the ramifications of becoming a single income household with similar fixed expenses. It's also important to identify any new items that will be added to the budget, like additional child care costs or counseling. Also, consider factoring in any alimony and child support payments, and the tax consequences or deductibility of each.

Just as you would with any other major life event, it's a good idea to put major purchases on hold and avoid unnecessary expenses. Also, try not to take on additional debt. This can keep you from coming out the other end of the divorce in bad financial shape and even save you from having to file bankruptcy.

Some divorcees choose to keep their homes to maintain some semblance of stability for their kids. Others decide to downsize to reduce costs and start anew. Renting for a little while might also work well for you. This would give you a moment to breathe and assess your financial situation before committing to a new home.

If you or your ex decide to keep the house, consider refinancing to have the other party taken off the loan. If the loan can't be refinanced, you or your ex can sign an agreement to continue to co-own the house for a specified period. However, doing so may hinder the chances for both of you to qualify for another mortgage.

Many times as you scale back your budget, you also reduce or completely eliminate insurance coverages to save on costs. This can be detrimental to your financial future because these coverages are designed to protect you from a major catastrophe. While it seems as if an extra $50 or $100 per month might be better spent on other items in your budget, the sense of security that these policies can provide is priceless.

Since your household now solely relies on your ability to produce a paycheck, maintaining and maybe even increasing your disability coverage is vital. Imagine your financial situation if you became disabled and could no longer take care of your expenses. You're now on your own, for better or for worse, and you need to plan accordingly.

As you review your insurance coverage, take the time to update your beneficiaries. Consider changing life insurance beneficiaries and those named on retirement accounts as well. It's a good idea to update your overall estate plan too. Review your will, guardianship elections, and even who you named as power of attorney and health care proxy. Many of these will still be in the name of your ex, so it's vital to update this as soon as you can if you don't want them involved in your end of life decisions.

One often overlooked area of your financial strategy is creating and funding your retirement plan. Coming out of your divorce may have slowed progress toward your retirement goals, but it's important to take stock of where you are and understand how to move forward. You may have used a QDRO to split retirement assets and now have your own accounts setup. Try not to tap into these accounts for anything other than retirement expenses. You may incur major taxes and penalties if you do. Instead, try to find room in your budget to contribute.

It's also important to understand the rules surrounding any pension or social security income you are eligible to claim when you retire. Sometimes, even though you are no longer married, you may be able to access your ex's retirement benefits. The Social Security Administration has some strict guidelines for these claims, so make sure you consult an expert.

Create a retirement plan to coordinate all your asset and income sources and to understand if you're on track to hit your goals. If not, the plan will help you to uncover what's needed to get you there. Whether you need to save more, work longer, or adjust your retirement lifestyle, you'll have a sense of security knowing that you're taking an active role in improving your financial future.

If you haven't filed for divorce yet but are about to, consider opting for a collaborative law divorce. If you and your soon-to-be ex want a civil procedure with low costs, then choosing this process might be best. A collaborative law divorce settles the dissolution of a marriage to best meet the specific needs of both parties and their children, all without the underlying threat of litigation. Both parties will need to sign a document committing to the process and agreeing to forgo any future litigation. Consider this as an alternative to the more traditional route of filing for divorce because it can save you money and aggravation.

Once you have been divorced for a while, you might find someone new that you'd like to marry. If you remarry, there are a variety of implications to consider. Some pension and retirement programs will stipulate that if you remarry, you may forfeit some or all your benefits that you would have received from your ex. This can be a rude awakening if you had been counting on this income as part of your retirement plan and don't find out until it's too late.

Also, stepchildren may enter the picture in a remarriage situation. If something were to happen to you and your new spouse, you would probably want your money to go to your own children rather than your stepchildren. Proper estate planning will ensure that your wishes are carried out in the event of your passing.

Imagine a situation where you pass away first and you have elected for all your money to go to your new spouse. After all, you want to make sure they are taken care of as well. If your spouse passes away soon after you and their beneficiaries are their own kids, you may have accidently disinherited your own children. To avoid this, you may opt for setting up a trust where you control the beneficiaries of the assets and you can ensure that the right people receive your money.

Same-Sex Couples

In 2015, the US Supreme Court legalized same-sex marriage and changed the way our country treats same-sex couples. As you might imagine, this change has huge financial planning implications if you are a member of the lesbian, gay, bisexual, and transgender (LGBT) community.

For starters, the federal government now recognizes gay marriage as a constitutional right. This includes the right to file your taxes jointly. Same-sex couples above a certain income threshold may face the "marriage penalty," so make sure you seek advice from your tax advisor on the best way to file your taxes.

You also have spousal rights to retirement programs. A same-sex spouse can make a traditional or Roth IRA contribution on behalf of a nonworking spouse, provided the couple files a joint return. Additionally, same-sex spouses who inherit a traditional or Roth IRA from their partner may rollover the inherited retirement account to their own traditional or Roth IRA as well as treat the inherited IRA as their own. Furthermore, younger spousal beneficiaries may establish an inherited IRA and delay receiving required distributions until the original IRA holder would have attained age 70 ½. This allows access to the retirement funds penalty free in the event the surviving spouse is under age 59 ½.

While perhaps not immediately apparent, the wage gap in America can significantly influence a same-sex couple's financial situation. As mentioned earlier, the Bureau of Labor Statistics has found that women tend to earn $0.79 for every $1.00 earned by a man. Because of this, lesbian couples can be dramatically disadvantaged compared to their heterosexual or even gay counterparts. This impacts both their household budgets and retirement savings. Lesbian couples may need to save a larger percentage of their salaries or work longer to fund the same financial goals as other couples. At the same time, if you're a part of a gay couple, you might have an advantage because both partners may earn one hundred cents on the dollar.

The Late Bloomer and the DINK

Many Americans don't start to review their financial situation and goals until they marry or have children. It's a turning point in your life when you are no longer responsible only for yourself, and it might make you think of the world in a different light. Since people are waiting longer and longer to get married, and sometimes choosing not to marry at all, they delay and avoid their financial preparation.

When it comes to saving for retirement, one of the biggest concepts that helps you accumulate wealth is compound interest. The earlier you begin saving, the faster interest can compound on itself. By delaying financial decisions based on planning, you may lose out on the benefits of this compounding. Do yourself a favor and start early, even if you save only a small amount. Your older self will thank you.

If you were to ask a 30-year-old single individual how much life or disability insurance they need, they probably would say that they don't need much. People typically purchase these insurances to support dependents who rely on them financially. By delaying marriage and children, the date when people obtain insurance can be pushed into the future, causing increased premiums due to increased age and potentially lower health ratings. Some people may not even qualify for coverage if their health has declined drastically. If you purchase insurance at a younger age, your insurance may cost less and you will gain early peace of mind.

As you age, you might find yourself wanting to have children. Imagine you decide to have a child in your 40s or even in your 50s. Whether you decide to conceive a baby naturally with your partner, opt for in vitro fertilization, or choose to adopt, it might be hard for you to manage all the competing financial priorities. You might be earning your highest income ever, yet at the same time be torn between opposing financial goals. You might even be retired by the time your kids attend college. You must consider a variety of factors if you decide to raise children later in life.

If you don't have children and aren't planning on starting a family, you face a different set of financial priorities. The term DINK or Dual Incomes with No Kids has been popularized lately. These families have a different set of financial issues. For couples who decide against raising kids, planning for retirement and the disposition of assets can get quite creative. Since childless couples will presumably not pass their wealth to the next generation, many times they give assets to siblings, nieces, and nephews. This is also a great opportunity to fund a favorite charity.

Be careful not to overlook planning for each other though. Just because you don't have any kids doesn't mean you should forget life, disability, and long term care insurances. You still want to protect the lifestyle you've created for your spouse and other family members.

Widows and Non-Parent Guardians

You may find yourself a member of one of the other types of family arrangements. Perhaps you are a widow who may or may not have had children. The emotional stress of losing a loved one can be quite painful. While handling this transition, make sure you can easily access pertinent financial documents and accounts.

Maybe you're old-fashioned and have a green hardbound book with a handwritten listing of everything. Or maybe you have everything stored digitally or in cloud-based software. You might even work with a financial advisor who oversees everything and can help you change over account titling and claim life insurance benefits; your advisor may even give you a checklist of things to do moving forward.

Now that it's just you, make a plan and start over in creating your financial goals. Similar to a divorce, you should take stock of where you are now and what you may need to alter to achieve your financial goals. You may also consider working with a tax advisor to ensure you properly claim the right filing status.

What if you are a non-parent guardian? Maybe your brother and sister-in-law passed away tragically, and you are now their children's guardian. Or perhaps you're a grandparent taking care of a grandchild. Whatever the situation, hopefully you knew before they passed that they had named you as the guardian. You likely felt honored by their trust, but you might not have asked many questions concerning this role.

Before accepting such a responsibility, you might want to ask how much life insurance they have and what assets they earmarked for their kids. Also, if there is a certain amount that they wanted allocated for specific expenditures, like a wedding or a down payment on a house. Maybe they set up trusts or other estate planning tools to facilitate the process. All these items would help you cover the added costs of caring for the children and not add undue financial pressures to your household. Without these established items, you might be putting your own financial goals on hold if you ever gain guardianship.

You also will want to know any particular wishes those parents want you to carry out. Did they want their kids to work during school to cover incidentals? Did they plan to cover the entire cost of college? What key financial habits would they have wanted their children to learn? All these items and more are good to discuss when having that conversation.

If you and your family fall into one of the above categories, you are now in the country's majority and traditional financial advice may not apply to you in the same way. Make sure to sit down with a financial professional who can help you learn how to achieve financial freedom.

Chapter 19
Employees in Transition

I never did a day's work in my life. It was all fun.
—Thomas Edison

Beginning in the second half of the 20th century, there was a monumental shift in the American workforce. Once there was a time when we began working for a company as young adults and worked our way up the corporate ladder. We'd spend our entire careers at one company holding a variety of different positions, each building upon the next. Times have changed, however, and workplace loyalty has vanished.

According to the Bureau of Labor Statistics, the average American worker will hold 11.7 jobs between the ages of 18 and 48 years old. Forrester Research predicts that today's youngest workers will hold 12 to 15 jobs in their lifetime.[41] With this much turnover, it's no wonder people struggle to handle their finances during times of transition.

You may decide to leave your job for a variety of reasons. Maybe you trade your government job for one in the private sector. You

---

[41] Alison Overholt, "Creating a Gem of a Career," Fast Company, 2012, accessed December 09, 2016. https://www.fastcompany.com/55827/creating-gem-career.

might leave a Fortune 500 company in favor of your dream job at a small firm, or better yet, to open up your own company. Conversely, you might move in a completely different direction and choose to stay home and manage the household, or take a short sabbatical from the 9-to-5 grind. In any of these situations, you can make specific preparations in your financial plan to give you confidence that the decisions you're making can be carried out without dramatically impacting your financial goals.

Retirement Plan Options

When you leave your job, you might debate about what you should do with the retirement plan held at the old job. After all, this is your retirement nest egg; you don't want it to be mishandled or abandoned. Most retirement plans offer four different options. Review each approach carefully and ensure that your decision aligns with your goals.

- **Withdraw the Funds**

There are many items to consider as you decide what do with your old retirement plan. You may decide, for whatever reason, that you'd like to take the money out of the plan and spend the proceeds. If you are younger than 59 ½, then it might not be best to cash out the plan. You'll pay considerable taxes and penalties for doing so and lose the opportunity cost of potential growth.

- **Keep It Where It Is**

Assuming you don't need the funds, then you may consider keeping the account at your old job. While this is the easiest choice since it requires nothing of you, it is not always advisable. As you change jobs over the course of your career, you may accumulate a few of these accounts in different places. They may become hard to oversee, and the investments inside the accounts may not align with your objective.

Sometimes, you may be forced to transfer your plan. If you hold a small balance in your account, the plan trustees might not want to maintain your account due to administrative fees and fiduciary liability.

- **Roll It into Your New Plan**

You may consider rolling your old plans into your newest job's retirement account. While it seems nice to consolidate all your accounts into one plan at your new job, there may be some limitations as well. Most employers will allow rollovers, but some may not, so make sure to check the plan's provisions to see if you can. Also, the investment lineup may be limited to the selection made by the fiduciaries. This may or may not be the right fit for you.

- **Roll It into an IRA**

If you're looking for a platform that allows freedom in fund selection, while still preserving the tax benefits of your old plan, it might make sense to roll your plan into an IRA. You may also decide to work with an advisor to design a balanced portfolio that is in line with your risk tolerance and time horizon.

Employee Benefits

As you transition jobs or retire from the workforce completely, one of the most important parts of the transition is understanding your employee benefits. The benefits of your prior job can differ from those offered at your new one. Employer-provided benefits are a key piece of your financial puzzle. With proper planning, you'll maximize everything available to you and won't leave any money on the table.

- **New Retirement Plan**

We've already discussed considerations for your old retirement plan, but what about your new one? Take the time to understand all your new plan's features, especially if your company matches your contribution. If they do, you will want to understand the vesting schedule for the employer contributions.

Companies have the right to take back all or a portion of the match they gave you if you leave before the contributions vest. A typical vesting schedule will give you rights to 20% of the employer contributions each year you stay with the company. After five years with the company, you are fully vested and can call the matching dollars your own. It's a good idea to know this as you decide to enter the plan.

If you're comfortable with the vesting requirements and you have additional cash flow, consider contributing to the plan to maximize the match. This is free money from your company, so you should take advantage of it. You'll also want to review the investment selection available with the new plan. Consider suitable investments in the plan and then coordinate the investments within your IRAs.

If you're fortunate enough to have a pension plan, you'll have some major factors to consider. Pension plans used to be the primary retirement plan used by employers to help employees finance their retirement. They defined the benefits you'd receive when you retire, which usually would be a percentage of your salary. These plans have been eliminated over the years in favor of programs like 401(k) plans, which allow the employer and employee to define the contributions made to the plan. This shift put greater risk and responsibility on the employee to contribute the optimal amount and manage the balance appropriately.

As you leave an employer that offered a pension plan, consider how much of your defined retirement income will be lost. Many pension plans calculate benefits based on years of service, as well as the average of your highest salary years. When you leave your job, you will no longer earn service credits and will lock in your salary for the calculation. This may result in a much lower pension payout than if you had stayed at your employer.

Often we can justify this decision since there may be a higher salary at the new job. This could greatly offset any lost pension income if the extra funds were invested. While the sentiment is a good one, we're not always disciplined enough to put the money away for the future.

As salaries rise, many people adjust their standard of living upward and forget to save the differential. This is where it pays to be a disciplined investor. If the money is not invested—or not wisely invested—then your retirement plan may be worse off than before you made the job change. Consider these factors carefully as you evaluate your options.

- **Health Insurance**

After you review your retirement plan options, your next concern will probably be how to handle your health insurance since most people obtain their health insurance through an employer.

If you plan on leaving the workforce altogether, you may decide to enroll in health insurance through your spouse's plan, if available. You may also choose to purchase health insurance privately or keep your old plan through COBRA. Keep in mind that since your employer may have been subsidizing some of the premiums, costs could be higher than expected.

If you plan to start a new job, consider when the new plan will go into effect. In some cases, you may find yourself with a gap in coverage. Your new plan may not start for a few weeks or even months after your old plan terminates. Consider working with your new company's HR department to see if they can be flexible on your start date. Beginning your new job a few days before the end of the month may allow you to qualify for benefits on the first of the next month. If this doesn't work out, consider purchasing short-term health insurance to cover the specific number of days you will be missing insurance. Premiums are significantly cheaper than COBRA, but benefits may not be as robust.

After plugging any gaps in coverage, it's time to set up your new plan. Your new company may offer only a limited selection of insurance plans, so you might need to compromise in some areas. Your doctors may or may not participate with the new insurance provider, so be sure to understand your options. Consider the benefits and costs of each plan and whether you have any upcoming significant health events. This will help in choosing the right plan that fits your needs.

Make sure you know when you're allowed to change the plan too. Oftentimes, open enrollment takes place in the fall, just before plans go into effect for the new year. It's a good idea to know this as you make your selection since you could select a plan that fits you now and change it later based on upcoming health expenses.

For example, let's say you enroll in your health plan midway through the calendar year. You know that you will incur some upcoming health-related expenses but not until next year. You may choose a less expensive plan now and then increase the plan's benefits during open enrollment for the following year. This could save you some considerable money today while allowing you to select coverage for foreseeable health expenses.

- **Life Insurance**

Another employee benefit that you'll probably leave behind as you transition out of your old job is group life insurance. Sometimes these plans are not transferable between jobs. You may have had a life insurance plan that gave you a multiple of your salary, or even bought into a group plan to buy-up your coverage. Either way, it's a good idea to review your coverage during this time.

Even if your new job offers you group life insurance, it might be wise to purchase a policy outside your company. This way you can lock in your rates today and not have to worry that your coverage is limited to the offering of your company.

If you end up leaving the workforce altogether, life insurance coverage may still be important to the household. Often people think that because they no longer generate income, they no longer need life insurance coverage. This couldn't be further from the truth.

Take Ruth for example. Ruth works as a teacher and has decided to exit the workforce temporarily to raise her two children. Even though Ruth doesn't generate income for the family, she has a full-time job managing the operations of the household.

If Ruth were no longer around, it would devastate the family, both emotionally and financially. Her husband would need to hire a full-time nanny or send the children to daycare. Life insurance can play a critical role in preventing financial distress during such a trying time.

- **Beneficiaries**

Many times when people leave a job or start a new one, their beneficiaries on their employee benefits are not in line with their estate plan. As you've bounced from one job to another, you may have made elections on your retirement plans and life insurance policies that have since become outdated.

The 401(k) from your first job might still have your parents as beneficiaries, while another job may list your spouse or children. Consider updating these to reflect your current family situation and your estate documents.

Cash Flow

During times of uncertainty and change, having a finger on the pulse of your household budget can help you navigate the shifting waters. Whether the decision to leave the workforce was your choice or outside of your control, being prepared with a large emergency reserve will give you the sense that you'll be able to keep your head above water. Experts recommend saving three to six months of expenses in liquid cash reserves in case you can't pay your bills with your paycheck. That number of months may increase for those individuals with variable income careers, like real estate agents or other sales professionals.

If you've been laid off and will no longer bring in a paycheck, it's a good idea to understand any severance packages that will be offered to you. Combine these funds with your emergency reserves, and it should give you a sense of how urgent the search for your next job is.

Knowing your monthly budget will also help in case you cannot work due to a disability or some other health-related illness or injury. Claiming on available disability benefits can stretch those reserves out much longer and give you a much-needed sense of security.

What if you're going out on maternity or paternity leave? You'll want to review your company's policies to see what's covered. If those months end up going unpaid, you'll want to know this ahead of time so you can avoid any surprises and keep you out of credit card debt.

Maybe you're thinking of taking a longer leave of absence to care for your new bundle of joy. Take a good long look at your budget to gauge the feasibility of running your household on a single income. Be sure to factor in baby expenses too, like diapers, wipes, and formula. Don't forget about increased health insurance costs now that you'll need to make sure your little one's covered under your plan.

It also wouldn't be a bad idea to give yourself a little bit of wiggle room too. As with any major life change, nothing goes exactly as you plan it. Padding your budget with a couple extra dollars per month will help ensure that you'll be able to manage any unforeseen expenses.

Ultimately, if things get too tight, consider opting for a part-time job. Some home-based businesses are easy to manage. They can give you a place to invest your non-baby time. It can also provide some extra income that can make a big difference to your monthly budget. Who knows, that hobby or small business might turn into a second career that will fuel your post-baby years.

One other important transition is that of a permanent exodus from the job market. To have the best chance of success for a sustainable retirement plan, create a well thought out budget. This will help bring confidence to an otherwise stressful situation. Saying goodbye to your biweekly paycheck can be quite emotional so be sure to have a plan that will keep you focused while also taking into consideration any surprise expenses.

Whether you're navigating a job change or going through some other major life event, transitions can be scary. You might find yourself panicking and conjuring up scary "what if" scenarios. With proper planning, those "what if's" can become "so what's." Your plan will act as a safety net for many of life's uncertain times. You'll be able to rest easy knowing everything will be alright in the end.

Chapter 20
The Missing Puzzle Piece

Don't quit. Never give up trying to build the world you can see, even if others can't see it. Listen to your drum and your drum only. It's the one that makes the sweetest sound.
—Simon Sinek

Close your eyes. Take a deep breath. Imagine that you've just found out that your long-lost Uncle Heathcliff has passed away. While you'd never met him, he bequeathed his entire fortune to you. It's more money than you could ever dream of having. It's enough money for you to be set for life, and then some.

What would you do? Would you quit your job? Go on a shopping spree? Travel the world? Think about all the things you would do with this money. Now, flash forward six months. The initial euphoria has worn off. What would you do now? How will this money change your life? Who will you become?

While this is only a fantasy right now, with proper planning and execution, it can become reality. You might not be able to quit your job and travel the world tomorrow. At the same time, small tweaks to your daily habits can place you closer to your financial goals. A little bit can go a long way.

Creating a financial plan is the first step to turning your dreams into a reality. The plan should help you organize and prioritize your objectives while staying on purpose. Ultimately it will align your habits and behaviors to help you to achieve success.

Find Your Why

If you were asked what the most important thing is to you, what would you say? Next consider why you say that? What is it about your answer that makes it the most important thing in your life? Now, ask yourself if the financial decisions you make speak to your most important thing.

Many people have a hard time with this concept. Finding only one thing that's most important to you can be daunting. At the same time, it is critical to ensuring that all your financial pieces are fit together in the right way for you. Each financial product or solution has its merits. The key to completing your financial puzzle is to review each piece and see where it might fit. Consider whether these products are furthering your goals or just distractions.

Let's take Harold for example. The most important thing in Harold's life is his children. Everything he does is to create a better life for his kids than he had. He wants to leave a legacy, not just in dollars but in morals and principles as well. Harold has a strong connection with his personal *why*. The action steps in his financial plan show him exactly how to align his finances with his values.

One of Harold's top financial priorities is saving for a college education for his kids. He wants to help them avoid the burden of student debt. At the same time, he expresses a concern that his kids will become reliant on the "Bank of Dad." He teaches them the value of a dollar and finds ways to encourage financial discussions.

Harold also values the benefits of life insurance coverage. He buys a policy that will provide for his family if he were no longer around. The beneficiaries of the policy also coordinate with his estate plan. He has opted to create an ethical will to pass on the values and traditions that he hopes his family continues.

Retirement planning is also important to Harold. At age 60, he hopes to scale back the professional work he's doing and spend more time with his family. He wants to be there to help support his kids and grandkids but needs financial freedom to do this. He creates a retirement strategy that will fulfill his wishes.

Harold is also budget conscious and has good spending habits. Every financial decision he makes is screened through the filter of his personal *why*. His financial plan has reached a state of financial flow that brings him fulfillment and joy. He is financially confident and feels good that he's making smart financial decisions that fit his values and beliefs.

Harold's story can give us insight into creating our own financial plans. If we don't connect with our *why*, then we might never get on the right track despite our best intentions. Just like with any goal, it's important to start with the end in mind.

Sticking to the Plan

As you execute your plan, you'll go through a period of optimism and excitement. After all, you've created a path to getting everything you want out of life. If that doesn't energize you, what will?

Along the way, you're bound to run into some challenges too. It's not a question of *if* you'll fall off the horse, but *when*. Be proactive and come up with a game plan to get ahead of these trouble spots *before* you encounter them. Sometimes the act of planning is a goal in and of itself. This is where most people fail and bail on their plans. With a keen eye on the prize, course-correct the plan over and over, and move forward.

Make your finances habitual. It's so much easier to have your plan run on autopilot than having to remember to write a check each month. Deduct your savings from your paycheck or your bank account automatically. This way, you'll never see it, and saving will feel less painful. As with any habit, it will take a while for this to become routine. Cut yourself some slack and understand the life cycle of creating habits.

You might feel as if you're pedaling uphill with the wind in your face. Know that it's okay to feel this way, and you'll be ahead of the game. The winds will eventually change, and you'll be gaining traction again. You may even achieve some small successes that indicate your plan is working. Congratulate yourself for pushing through and keep moving forward.

Life is full of distractions. Try and anticipate them ahead of time to remain focused on your goals. Imagine you're at a dinner party. A friend approaches you and tells you about this new financial strategy. His opinions make you second-guess the plan you created. But then you remember that what works for him may not necessarily work for you. You leave confidently, knowing that the plan you created is the best fit for you.

Keep in mind that people like to talk about how great they're doing but never tell you about their struggles. Your friend might not be telling you about the credit card debt that keeps him up at night. Before taking any advice, look at it through the lens of what you're trying to achieve. Connect with your *why* and ask yourself if this advice is best suited for your situation. Better yet, bounce it off your financial planner. Otherwise, you'll end up running from one idea to the next and never getting anywhere.

Selecting a Financial Planner

As you may suspect, a plan is only as good as its implementation. Your financial success depends on proper planning and execution. If you find that your plan isn't working, determine if the problem is with the plan itself or in the execution. Sometimes, we make excuses for ourselves and let ourselves off the hook. That's where a financial planner comes in.

Hiring a financial planner is the last piece of your puzzle. As an accountability partner and coach, their job is to ensure that you carry out your plan. They're also available to help you amend the plan as your life changes. Sometimes a planner may even persuade you against actions that move you away from your goals.

During the 2008 financial crisis, some people acted on their fears and sold out of the market. Instead of selling out completely, these people could have dialed back their risk profile. For those with long-term horizons, staying the course would have been a better move. Keeping a level head during times of increased market volatility will keep your plan on track. Don't let the economy "out there" hold your economy "in here" hostage.

A planner might also help you put your financial goals into perspective. Believe it or not, some people actually save too much money for retirement. In situations like this, a planner can help you redirect your savings strategy toward other financial priorities.

As you make the decision to hire a trusted advisor, you'll want to review the various types. Each type has its pros and cons. It'll also help you to know how to select the right one for you.

- **Fee-Only Planners**

The fee-only planner charges a flat or hourly fee to provide financial advice. Since all their revenue comes from fees, their rates are higher than other types of planners.

For that reason, they can't help you select financial products since it's outside the scope of their fiduciary duties. While this might make them seem more impartial, many times a plan will not work out without advisor help. With fee-only planners, you'll need self-motivation to carry out plan recommendations on your own. You might even need to hire other advisors to help you buy products or open accounts.

- **Fee-Based Planners**

Fee-based planners earn both fees and commissions. You might hire this type of planner to help you create your plan first. After the plan is in place, you can then choose to work with them to select products or set up accounts. Any specific product recommendations are not a part of the plan, and you are under no obligation to follow them.

Fee-based planners have lower fees since they receive revenue from a variety of sources. This can be a more affordable way for you to create a financial plan. They can help guide you through the action steps in your plan and be a great accountability coach too.

- **Commission-Based Advisors**

Commission-based advisors provide financial services without a fee. Instead, they hope you will purchase products from them. As a result of your opening an account or buying a policy, they are paid a commission. This might help you get started working with an advisor since there are no upfront fees. At the same time, you may not get an unbiased, comprehensive look at your entire situation.

Regardless of the type of planner or advisor you consider, each has an individual business model. You should ask the planner how he or she is compensated. Good planners will be straightforward about how they receive payment for services. They should be able to define their relationship with you without hesitation.

Many organizations have been created to support the financial planning industry. At the forefront of the industry is the Certified Financial Planner Board of Standards. The CFP® Board has become the certifying body for the CFP® designation. This mark signifies that the planner has undergone extensive education and subscribes to a high standard of ethics.

As noted by the CFP® Board's Standard of Excellence, CFP® professionals "are obliged to uphold the principles of integrity, objectivity, competence, fairness, confidentiality, professionalism and diligence as outlined in CFP® Board's Code of Ethics. The Rules of Conduct require CFP® professionals to put your interests ahead of their own at all times and to provide their financial planning services as a 'fiduciary,' acting in the best interest of their financial planning clients."[42] This is important because you'll want to find a trusted and reliable place to receive your advice.

At the end of the day, selecting the right financial planner comes down to who you connect with the most. Reviewing your personal financial situation can get emotional. You might discuss your attitudes toward money and habits that you've created over the years. You may even uncover some hidden resentments. Feeling comfortable as you discuss the good, the bad, and the ugly will go a long way.

Your Life, Your Plan

Once you've selected your planner and put a plan in place, you're now on your way to living your life on purpose. You'll have created a state of financial flow, balancing saving for tomorrow and spending for today. Furthermore, you'll have reviewed worst case scenarios and created contingency plans for emergencies.

Most important of all, you will have aligned your money with your values. The decisions you make each day will be in harmony with who you are and what you believe in. The legacy you leave won't just be monetary, but also in values and traditions. The life you lead and the actions you take will speak louder than any words. Your children will see you as a role model and aspire to learn from your successes.

Money doesn't buy happiness. But, treat it right, and you'll live a financially free life. You'll be free to focus more time, energy, and soul on your purpose. This will help you become your best version of yourself. You'll spend less time worrying and arguing about money and more time on your personal why. Which, in the end, may just be the meaning of life. So, go forth and conquer. Godspeed.

---

[42] "About CFP Board," Ethics and Enforcement - CFP Board, accessed December 09, 2016, http://www.cfp.net/about-cfp-board/ethics-enforcement.

Index

About the Author

Jason Silverberg specializes in comprehensive financial planning. His practice aims at helping individuals, families, and small business owners create new financial visions, opportunities, and futures while overcoming obstacles that may hinder success.

Jason takes a values-based approach, which allows him to connect with his clients on a deeper level, diving into the *why* behind the numbers. He focuses on helping clients achieve and protect their goals through methodical investment strategies, calculated risk management, and insurance solutions.

Continuing education is key to Jason's thirst for knowledge. He is a CFP® (Certified Financial Planner™) professional and has received his CLU® (Chartered Life Underwriter) and ChFC® (Chartered Financial Consultant) designations from The American College of Financial Services.

Jason appeared on ABC's *The Savvy Investor Show* and is a regular financial speaker at the United States Patent & Trademark Office. Additionally, he was a financial correspondent for *Take Pride Community Magazine*.

Jason lives in Gaithersburg, MD with his wife, Lindsay, and his children, Joshua and Rebecca. He enjoys running outside and participating in competitive races. He completed the Frederick Marathon in 2010 and participates annually in the Kentlands/Lakelands 5K.

Jason is a registered representative and investment advisor representative of Securian Financial Services, Inc., Member FINRA/SIPC. Financial Advantage Associates, Inc. is independently owned and operated.

Greetings!

Thank you so much for completing *The Financial Planning Puzzle*! It was truly an honor to write this book for you, and I hope you enjoyed it. If so, please share this book with a friend or loved one!

I'd love to hear from you too! Please send me an e-mail at jason@finadvinc.com or call me at 301-610-0071 with any thoughts or personal financial questions you have. I can help you solve your own financial planning puzzle and achieve your financial goals.

Along with the rest of the book bonuses, I've included a FREE mini-course on the 5 Steps to Solving Your Financial Planning Puzzle. You can use this bonus to enhance the book's experience by putting the concepts to work to help you achieve your goals.

You can find that at **www.bit.ly/fppbookbonus**. It's packed with great tools and resources to help you begin your journey to financial success.

Thanks again for reading the book. I look forward to connecting with you soon!

Warm Regards,

Jason Silverberg

In addition to being an author and a financial planner for his clients, Jason presents a seminar series that coordinates with the book. These presentations are designed to take a more in-depth look at some of the financial pieces and the unique ways of fitting them together. Some of the topics include:

> **5 Steps to Solving Your Financial Planning Puzzle (Signature Keynote)**

> **Life Insurance: Are you Protected?**

> **21st Century Investment Strategies**

> **Business Solutions and Succession Plans**

If you would like to hire Jason to speak at your next event, please call 301-610-0071 or email him at jason@finadvinc.com.

CPSIA information can be obtained
at www.ICGtesting.com
Printed in the USA
LVOW09*0742070317
526358LV00017B/443/P